The Purple Spoon

The story of a cook, writer and self-publisher

by Lazy Cook Mo Smith

®

The Purple Spoon

Published in November 2006

by

Lazy Cook Mo Smith
Bear House
Bisley
Stroud, Glos. GL6 7BB
Email: info@lazycookmosmith.co.uk
Website: www.lazycookmosmith.co.uk

ISBN 0-9542319-5-3

Written by Lazy Cook Mo Smith

Cover design by Terry Cripps, Saul, Gloucestershire
Typesetting by David Onyett, Cheltenham, Gloucestershire
Printed by Leckhampton Printing Co. Cheltenham,
Gloucestershire

to

Yvonne

Written and Published by the same author
'A Lazy Cook's Christmas'
ISBN 0954231929
Price £4.99 per copy

'Lazy Cook in the Kitchen'
ISBN 0954231910
Price £6.99 per copy

'A Lazy Cook's Summer'
ISBN 0954231902
Price £6.99 per copy

'The Lazy Cook's Favourite Food'
ISBN 0954231945
Price £8.99 per copy

Available from

Lazy Cook Mo Smith
Bear House
Bisley
Stroud, Glos. GL6 7BB

All prices include p/p
(cheques made payable to Lazy Cook Mo Smith)
Buy online
Website: www.lazycookmosmith.co.uk
A percentage of each sale is given to charity

Acknowledgements

With grateful thanks to

Liz Petheram
Helen Sundaram
Annie Fell
Nicky Rogers
Charlie Walker

Donations made to the following charities:

Age Concern
Air Ambulance, Gloucester
Bisley Flower Show, Bisley, Glos.
Bisley Village Hall Committee
Christian Aid

CLIC – Children with Leukaemia
Cotswold Care Hospice – Minchinhampton, Glos.
CWR overseas fund
Disasters Emergency Committee
Fiery Beacon, Glos.

MacMillan Nurses
Made in Stroud, Stroud, Glos.
Rafe Fund, Glos.
Riding for the Disabled
RSPCA

Stroud Beresford Group, Stroud, Glos.
Stroud Choral Society, Stroud, Glos.
Tearfund
The Door – Stroud, Glos.
Treloar Trust

Cooking is like Christianity –
the simpler it is,
the more nourishing it is.

The Purple Spoon

The story of a cook, writer and self-publisher

Contents

Introduction   1

Part 1
A Bee in my Bonnet   3

Part 2
From Cooker to Computer   103

Index   230

Introduction

A large purple melamine spoon seemed a remarkable gift to receive from a lady of nearly 90 years. Francie was the maiden aunt of my husband, Adam. Many years retired from her career as a masseuse and a founder member of the Chartered Society of Physiotherapy she was now living in a residential home on the outskirts of Birmingham and often came to us for Sunday lunch.

This large melamine spoon – the latest fashion icon in kitchen cuisine – took pride of place in the painted jam jar which housed the tools I regularly used when preparing meals. Adam and I had been recently married and after many years of flat sharing, for the first time in my life I had a kitchen I could call my own.

Part One

A BEE IN MY BONNET

The first time that I can remember experimenting with ingredients, which to me is what cooking is all about, was the year the family had been given for Christmas a large box of chocolates, the sort shops had and weighed out into small cone-shaped greaseproof bags. After our initial enjoyment of these chocolates, which were an absolute luxury as chocolates were still rationed after the war years, the box was placed at the foot of the stairs. That holiday I spent a lot of time 'playing' in my parents' bedroom. Taking a selection of the remaining chocolates, I returned to the bedroom, removed the centres and mixed them before replacing them into the chocolate cases. Why I did this I do not remember, but, the proof of the pudding is in the eating and I ate a lot of chocolates. You might imagine the trouble I was in when the somewhat depleted box was found!

I was born in January 1937 and brought up in West Bromwich in the heart of the Black Country where I lived with my parents, two elder sisters, Audrey and Elsie and my Grandma Woodhall (Gran), in a small council house on the edge of a housing estate.

At the age of five years I started school at the Greets Green Board School – not to be confused with a boarding school! I vaguely remember one morning sitting an examination which, to the great disappointment of my parents, I failed and as a result my education continued from the age of 11 at the George Salter Secondary Modern School at the top of Claypit Lane.

I disliked this new school intensely and did everything I possibly could to get out of going. I would frequently arrive home at lunchtime pretending to have a headache or a stomach ache and I must have been quite a good little actress because on these occasions I always managed to get the sympathy of my Mother or my Gran and an afternoon at home was assured!

The main reason for my dislike of school was the difficulty I had with reading. I never actually admitted this to anyone but my school reports always included the comment, 'a poor reader.' This didn't seem to worry my parents, if anything they chose to ignore it and never encouraged me to read at home. From memory, apart from children's books, the only book at home was the large family Bible which my Father would sometimes read to us. I couldn't ignore this because it accounted for most of the unhappy days I spent at school.

Being a poor reader can be a handicap in so many ways. I was also a very slow reader and when given a chapter of a book to read to ourselves after which we would be given questions to answer I would get into an awful mess. If I tried to read quickly I would miss out so many words that the text didn't make sense but if I read at my normal snail's pace I got very behind but as soon as I noticed the girl next to me turning a page I would turn a page even though I hadn't read it all. Consequently when it came to answering the questions I hadn't a clue what to write with the result that I was nearly always at the bottom of the class. I don't ever remember being questioned about my reading difficulties; word blindness and dyslexia were unheard of all those years ago. My sentences never flowed smoothly and in my anxiety I would read words out of sequence or add words which were not printed. Words of more than two syllables would leave me completely tongue-tied. Reading, to say the least, was a real pain to me just as listening to my ramblings must have been to others. My teacher seemed totally insensitive to my dilemma, if anything she would often aggravate it. I well remember the occasion when, during the class reading of a particular novel, to my distress, I heard my name being called to read the next paragraph. The very thought of being asked to read aloud in class could make me physically sick. On this occasion my usual plan to hide behind the girl in front of me with my head well down in the hope that I might not be noticed, failed. When my teacher called my name again I realised there was no escape. With knees knocking and my whole body feeling like a wobbly jelly, I rose to my feet. The girl preceding me had read so beautifully emphasising each word with real feeling and understanding. Words rolled off her tongue like dramatic cloud formations on a windy day as she set the scene and described the main characters in the story, I had been entranced. The book we were reading was written in dialect. For me, to be asked to stand up and read the most simple script was a problem, but to read dialect aloud would, I knew, be an impossibility. As I stammered and stumbled through the first few words I was conscious of the giggles from my classmates over which my teachers voice shouted, "For goodness sake child, what are you saying? Pull yourself together and start again." I never remember feeling more humiliated in my life.

I was no good at games either. All manner of academic inadequacies are overlooked if you can score for your team. Netball was our team game but I rarely caught the ball and if I did I surprised myself so much that I immediately dropped it, I was a real 'butter fingers'.

But there were other reasons why I disliked school. Unlike today's youngsters, at the age of 11 and 12 we were still innocent little girls… even so, physical changes were becoming evident. As I looked around I noticed these changes taking place in most of my classmates. They were all shaping up rather nicely and in all the right places. I was still little, thin and with legs up to my bottom, as my Father often said. My only curve was on the end of my nose about which I was often teased.

I also noticed that waves of blonde or brown hair caressed their shoulders and soft curls framed their pretty faces. My hair was black with a copper sheen which I hated. It was also as straight as a die. My sisters, Audrey and Elsie, had been blessed with the curls I longed for. I remember as a very young child, before I started school, nearly burning the house down trying to curl my locks. I would be mesmerised as I watched my Gran put curling irons into a flame of the cooker. After a while she removed them, pinched them between wetted fingers which resulted in a sizzling noise before wrapping her hair around them. The result was frizzy curls framing her face. I wanted these frizzy curls and noticing a comb on the mantelpiece one day, I put it into the open fire. When I removed it in flames I threw it on to the coconut matting which immediately caught fire and I ran into the kitchen to my Mother. I was given a smacked bottom and told I was a naughty little 'faggit' (a Black Country expression for a naughty child). In later years I would attach my Mother's metal waving clips to my hair before going to bed but those which didn't fall out on to my pillow left ugly lines of hair resembling railway tracks. If I could persuade her, my Mother would sometimes tie my hair in rags but she wasn't very good at this, became impatient and it ended in tears. The next morning the curls were disappointing and you could guarantee it was raining. Before I got to school my hair was straight again.

I also noticed that most of my classmates, and my sisters, had big brown or blue eyes. Mine were green, and they were covered, in fact practically the whole of my little face was covered, with the most enormous pair of N.H.S. spectacles!

For all these reasons I continued to dislike school, until one day my class was taken into the prefabricated building which had been erected in a corner of the playground. From the moment I entered that room I felt inquisitive and relaxed. It was a feeling I had never experienced at school.

This classroom was not only new but it was different from any classroom I had known. Instead of the familiar rows of desks and chairs, this room was divided into little kitchen areas each fitted out with a sink and a cooker, pots and pans and a work table. We were told we were going to have our very first Domestic Science lesson. Miss Jones, our Domestic Science teacher was tall, blonde and blue eyed with a willowy figure and I thought she was wonderful. During that first lesson I listened to every word she spoke and watched spellbound as she demonstrated how to cook to the class. Returning to my appointed kitchen area I put into practice what I had seen. By some miracle it worked and I produced results similar to those of the teacher. For the first time ever I watched as my classmates struggled with ingredients, burnt or cut their fingers and generally seemed to get into a muddle. This sudden and unexpected success gave me a new found confidence I had never experienced and I soon became very ambitious. Rock cakes and potato soup were child's play to me, I was impatient to move on to more adventurous things, to test my skills and show a little flair and imagination. It was almost as though overnight my thoughts had turned from the vanity of curls and shapely bodies to cooking, to creating wonderful flavours, presenting meals, to make them attractive to the eye and acceptable to the palate. My head was buzzing with ideas and I soon decided that when I grew up I would be a cookery demonstrator. Thinking back, I must have driven that young and newly qualified teacher scatty.

One day, at the end of one of these cookery classes as we called them, we were told that the education Inspectors would be visiting our school the following week and we were all to take special care over our appearance. We were to make sure our fingernails were short and clean, our hair tidy and our apron laundered. We were each given a recipe which we were to make during this important visit and we were to be sure to remember all the ingredients. I decided this was my big chance to show off my new found skills to someone other than my teacher who was never encouraging or complimentary about my cooking however hard I tried to impress her – could you blame her! Taking little notice of the recipe I had been given I produced a black and white picture of a cake and said, I am going to make this – the picture was of a Battenburg cake. Despite my teacher's instant objection I was determined to make it. Where I got this picture from I cannot to this day remember. It would not have been from my Mother who would never have been interested in, or had the time to read the type of magazine in which this delicacy would have featured, even if she could have afforded to buy it. At this time there were few magazines showing photographs of cakes of such a fancy variety. Most cookery books would have been the ones given when you bought a new cooker, or ones produced by manufacturers of flour and other basic ingredients and the recipes would have been of very simple, everyday meals. I do not remember where I obtained the specially shaped tin, the food colouring, the marzipan or any of the other specialist ingredients needed to produce such a confection, but I did. I carefully followed the instructions and, observing every detail in the picture, I made the most perfect Battenberg cake – just like the picture. However, my efforts appeared to go unnoticed by the inspectors. My teacher was so cross with me that she kept them well away from my working area. I have never made such a Battenburg cake since but people seem to enjoy my Chocolate Battenburg made more quickly from a Marble Cake mixture.

On another occasion each member of the class was given a project to research. I had to find out as much as I could about washing powders, polishes and dyes. We were told each project would be judged by the headmistress and the best would be awarded a prize which would be presented at assembly on the last day of term. I was really excited by this idea and, taking addresses from my Mother's packets and tins I wrote to the various manufacturers telling them all about my project and asking if they could help me. To my surprise and delight they each replied and sent posters and little sample tins and packets of their products. After carefully reading through all the handouts I wrote a brief history of each product. I spent hours writing and re-writing these notes using my Mother's dressing table as a desk and eventually I put together as colourful a project as I was able. The day they were judged the headmistress and teacher, followed by enthusiastic classmates, spent a lot of time examining my display and talking quietly together. An expectant atmosphere had built up around my table and I had never before felt so near to winning a school prize – I could hardly contain my excitement. But this premature euphoria was suddenly halted by the voice of the headmistress. Addressing her remarks to me she said, "I have to admit that your project is without doubt the best but, as your father has a shop." This was true; he did have a small shop selling groceries and general stores, "we feel you have had an unfair advantage over the rest of the class and we cannot award you first prize." I was disappointed beyond belief and my confidence was completely shattered. But my disappointment was short lived. Cooking was the only thing I was any good at so I was determined to succeed and one day become a cookery demonstrator.

School leaving age was 15 and just before the end of my final term accompanied by my Mother I was given an appointment to meet the careers officer. It was almost a foregone conclusion that every girl at my school would take a job either in a local factory or a shop. If you were really bright you might then be accepted to train as a telephonist or office girl. The interview seemed a mere formality to decide into which category each girl fitted. You might well imagine the surprise on the face of the careers lady when, in reply to her question, "what would you like to do?" I replied in a loud and clear voice, "I'm going to be a cookery demonstrator." For just a moment she was lost for words, then, regaining her composure she continued, "but you have no suitable qualifications, your education has not included the in depth study of the subjects needed to be a cookery demonstrator, I could not possibly recommend you for such a training." Minutes later I left that office with a highly embarrassed Mother and no job prospects, but, as my Father often said, I had a bee in my bonnet and was determined that one day I would be a cookery demonstrator. I did not realise at that moment the difficulties, the frustrations, the disappointments, the excitements and the pleasures I would encounter before I achieved this childhood ambition.

My Mother

My Gran

Myself aged 12 years

My sisters – Audrey (R), Elsie
and myself

Myself sewing in the garden
with Monty

My Father

Three months after leaving school I was sent, complete with specs, sister Audrey's oversized mackintosh and a broad Black Country accent, to the smartest secretarial college in Birmingham to learn shorthand and typing.

With the help of Denise Cox who had not come straight from a boarding or finishing school and who's Mummy didn't have a maid, but who befriended me from the start, I somehow survived the secretarial college and at the end of the nine month course I took my first job with a life assurance company in the centre of Birmingham. This gave me a little pocket money to spend as I liked, and I decided to save it and use it to get myself trained as a cookery demonstrator. I very soon discovered that this was not going to be as easy as I had imagined. On my visit to enrol at the City of Birmingham College of Food and Domestic Science, I learnt that there were no courses in the college syllabus for the training of cookery demonstrators. This was done by the Gas or Electricity Boards and before anyone was even considered for such a training by either boards, it was necessary to attend a two year day course at the college. This course not only covered all aspects of cookery from elementary to advanced recipes but also included studying the science of food, bookkeeping, housewifery and flower arranging. The more I heard the more I wanted to do this course but I also realised that, even if I could have afforded to give up my job to attend such a course, I would not have been accepted because I needed certain 'O' and 'A' level qualifications before my application could be considered. I had first heard of these 'O' and 'A' levels at secretarial college but I hadn't a clue what they were, but I kept quiet about this, even to Denise. Whatever they were I knew I hadn't got them and so I contented myself, for the time being, by enrolling for an evening class, the City and Guilds 233 Elementary Cookery Course held two nights a week, Monday and Thursday, from 6 pm. until 9 pm.

The classes took place in a large converted house on the Hagley Road near the junction with Portland Road. The kitchen was large and airy. Huge work tables were arranged down the centre and on each side were cookers, sinks and refrigerators. Deep shelves displayed an assortment of pots and pans of all shapes and sizes. Everything sparkled and was in 'apple pie order'. There was an air of professionalism about the place and for the second time in my life I felt completely at ease on entering that kitchen.

The class was made up of about a dozen students who to me, now in my late teens, appeared middle-aged, with the exception of Stella Spencer, whom I immediately befriended. I soon discovered that Stella was in her twenties and was engaged to Stanley Jones, a medical student at Birmingham University.

Our teacher, Mrs Paxton, was short and dark with a generous nature. She quickly gained the respect and admiration of the whole class. I lost no time in telling her about my intention to become a cookery demonstrator and she was the first person to listen and to encourage me in my ambition.

In my eagerness to learn I bubbled over with enthusiasm and energy though there were times when I was completely out of my depth. I was totally inexperienced compared with most of the class who had spent years cooking for their families and were familiar with basic everyday cooking. Stella, whom I discovered was a teacher at a private school in Edgbaston, showed clear signs of being much more able than me at cooking.

On the evenings when Mrs Paxton demonstrated, I listened to every word with absolute concentration and carefully observed her every movement. I used my shorthand to make endless notes which I spent hours writing into longhand and illustrating with sketches, before the next lesson.

There was so much to remember. I learnt that a wooden spoon was always used when stirring ingredients in a saucepan, a metal one made too much noise and damaged the base of the pan. The only wooden spoon we had at home was the very large one Mother used at Christmas to stir the puddings and the cake. I decided to purchase a set of wooden spoons of varying sizes out of my next wage packet. I learnt the importance of a stock pot and I learnt how to make a basic white sauce of pouring or coating consistency. This tasted very different from Mother's who occasionally made white sauce by mixing cornflour and cold milk to a smooth paste then stirring it into hot milk. This basic white sauce was made by melting butter in a pan and then adding 'plain' flour – another ingredient we didn't have at home. The butter and plain flour were stirred over a gentle heat until a smooth paste was formed and this paste was called a 'roux'. On to this roux was poured hot milk and stirring continued over the gentle heat until a smooth sauce of the desired consistency was made. The pronunciation of French words which were frequently quoted was an added headache to me, I hadn't studied French at my secondary modern school. I also learnt that gravy was not made with Bisto, an ingredient in daily use at home, and that bi-carbonate of soda was not added to the cabbage to keep its colour! I learnt that 'soup boiled is soup spoiled' and that scones are 'quick to make and quick to bake.' I was fascinated by it all and, although I was often slower than the remainder of the class, I was encouraged by the fact that I seemed to have no difficulty in remembering everything I was taught. When it came to the presentation of food, an aspect of cooking I really enjoyed, I showed endless patience ensuring that my dishes looked attractive and my presentation of them was original.

Throughout the course I was constantly being introduced to new dishes and I discovered how easy it was to make the most ordinary everyday ingredients into a delicious meal.

Cauliflower au gratin was one such example. We regularly ate plain boiled cauliflower at home but this was something very different, different even from the more rustic presentation of cauliflower cheese so popular today and, dare I say it, very different from my Lazy Cook Quick Cauliflower Cheese! Care was needed during the preparation and cooking of this recipe. The cauliflower must remain whole and be coated with a velvety smooth cheese sauce. The consistency of the sauce was important, it must not be of such a thickness that it clung to the pre-cooked cauliflower like a heavy blanket, or so thin that it left a naked cauliflower sitting in a pool of sauce. The right consistency ensured that it coated the cauliflower and a topping of fresh breadcrumbs, dotted with butter, completed the preparation before it was placed under a grill.

For the demonstration the teacher had used a special oven proof au gratin dish and because of my passion for good presentation, the use of the correct dish was as important to me as the cauliflower itself. I knew for certain we had nothing remotely resembling this dish at home, not even amongst the items in the best china cabinet, the contents of which, to my knowledge, were first used in celebration of my Uncle Jo returning home from the war, and thereafter on Christmas Days only. On my next pay day I went straight to Barrows, the smartest and most expensive shop in town, and bought a green Denby au gratin dish. At the end of the evening when all the completed dishes were displayed for Mrs Paxton's inspection and criticism, mine, the only one served in an au gratin dish, was described as a perfect example of good presentation. This was the very first time I could remember being congratulated on my efforts. I had spent nearly all my weekly wage on that dish but it had been worth it and now, many years later, it is still in regular use in my kitchen.

Tearing around a hot kitchen cooking and presenting beautiful dishes after a day's work was one thing, getting them home intact was another. I had three buses to catch and the journey took me two hours, longer if I was unfortunate enough to miss a bus connection. I would wait at cold, draughty bus-stops, often in pouring rain, conscious that my brown paper carrier bag was getting sodden and might tear under the strain but as both hands were usually full and my arms bulging with books or parcels there was nothing I could do about it. I would arrive home tired and cold. The family would be sitting around a glowing fire and would greet me with, "What have you made tonight? Get some plates and let's try it." At first their comments were anything but complimentary but as I progressed they became more encouraging and there often followed a request that I make that particular dish at home. Whether it was to please my family or to improve my skills I don't remember, but I do remember spending most weekends at the cooker which was situated in our glass verandah (called a conservatory now), where, in winter it was freezing cold, and in summer it was like a hot-house.

As the weeks passed my enthusiasm for cooking continued and my confidence increased. I loved every minute I spent at the evening classes. Even so there were many times when, in my ignorance, I made the most frightful mistakes and all the class had a good laugh at my expense. There were also times when my inexperience and lack of a basic knowledge of cooking gave me problems which left me completely deflated. One such occasion still remains vividly in my memory. We were given at least one prac-tical test each term, usually working on our own in preparation for the examination. These tests not only included the preparation, cooking and presentation of certain dishes but elaborate time sheets had to be made itemising every detail, minute by minute. It was likely, we were told, that an examiner would walk around the kitchen and look at our time sheet to check that we were not getting too behind. Furthermore, little labels had to be prepared to be placed by any leftover ingredients, stating how they would.be used another day – my Mother's motto, 'waste not, want not' often came to mind. For example, vegetables might be added to a soup, cake might be used for a trifle or crumbed and stored for future use. Nothing could be thrown away. In preparation for these tests I would do a dummy run at home the weekend before just to make sure everything I had planned worked and fitted into my time schedule.

One of these tests involved the planning and cooking of a three-course dinner for four people – dinner parties were just becoming fashionable in some homes, but not in ours. Mrs Paxton said it was too much for an individual to tackle in so short a time and it was too expensive for one person to budget for, so she had decided to put us into pairs. It came as a real disappointment to me when I heard my name paired off, not with Stella, who would have been my natural choice, but with the only member of the class I felt slightly ill at ease with.

On the night of the test I was terribly nervous and my very entry into the kitchen signalled calamity. Everything I attempted went wrong. I boiled the soup. I clumsily knocked my partner's perfectly shaped dinner rolls into the bowl of steaming water over which they were rising. I forgot to sieve the mashed potatoes which resulted in my partner being unable to squeeze them through the piping bag to shape them into duchesse potatoes, and I over whipped our only pot of double cream, reducing the planned party gateau to a naked jam sponge. Conscious that we were more than a little behind and sensing the anxiety of my partner amid the increasing chaos caused entirely by me, I nervously asked, "Is there anything I can do to help?" My partner immediately stopped what she was doing, looked at me for a moment and then said, "Oh, make the gravy." Make the gravy! she might just as well have asked me to fly to the moon. I had never made gravy in my life before and without the aid of my Mother's Bisto, I hadn't a clue how to begin. Despite me, we somehow survived the test. Thankfully it was only a test and not the real thing – I still had much to learn.

I started my homeward journey in tears and on that shaky old bus I relived the events of the evening. Soon my tears of frustration and inadequacy turned to tears of laughter as the humour of my errors unfolded and I was saved from giving up the course and letting that bee out of my bonnet.

Of course I continued to make many mistakes but I was quick to learn. I seemed to possess a natural ability when handling food and my presentation of ingredients was always original. I also received a great deal of encouragement from Mrs Paxton who was always interested in what I was doing. But when it came to the theory I was completely out of my depth and I soon realised my poor education was a tremendous handicap to me. Science and chemistry had played little part in my school education, as I remembered. However I gradually learned the importance of a basic knowledge of each of these subjects, especially the science of food when I was faced with words like amino acids, proteins, minerals, vitamins, carbohydrates, calories and many more. It was important to understand why certain ingredients had to be thoroughly cooked before they became acceptable to the palate and to the digestive system. I learnt about the changes which occurred when certain ingredients were cooked, for example flour and potatoes, I was told, needed to be cooked until the starch grains burst. Uncooked potatoes are indigestible. A sauce which has not been cooked for long enough will have an unpleasant flavour which will spoil a recipe. I read how the addition of a little vinegar to red cabbage would prevent it turning blue during cooking, blue is not a colour used in cooking. I was told of the importance of dissolving sugar crystals in a liquid before allowing them to reach boiling point. Failure to dissolve every grain will result in invert sugars and no amount of cooking, slowly or otherwise, will correct this. I ignored this to my cost in later years when attempting to make jam in a hurry.

The theory seemed endless and to me it was like trying to learn a foreign language when I felt I hardly knew the Queen's English. I had great difficulty understanding and keeping up with it but soon it became all too clear to me that knowing how to cook wasn't enough. If I was to pass the examination, the theory was equally important and without the elementary certificate I would be unable to go on to the advanced course and without this, I hadn't a chance of being considered for training as a cookery demonstrator, my one aim in life.

Stella had an elder sister, Marjorie Wood, who became as dear a friend as Stella. Marjorie had already completed the first year of the advanced course and told me a little of what this entailed. I was excited by the thought of the advanced dishes I might prepare but the thought of the advanced theory worried me no end. "A dietician has been brought in to lecture students on advanced science of food" said Margery. Oh dear, how would I cope with the understanding of the digestive system and special diets? But that was all in the future and I decided it was best not to look too far ahead but to take one step at a time.

Stella also knew of my ambition to become a cookery demonstrator and would sometimes accompany me to a Gas or Electricity Board demonstration. On these occasions I longed for the opportunity to step into the shoes of the demonstrator. I was sure my chance would come one day, perhaps sooner than I had expected. Mrs Paxton greeted me one evening saying she had met the person who appointed trainee demonstrators for the West Midlands Electricity Board and had talked to her about me. The result was that I was offered an interview. I was to be at the Electricity Board Headquarters in Mucklow's Hill, Halesowen at 2 pm. the following Wednesday – I could not believe my luck – what an opportunity! For the next week I could think of little but this interview and of its possible outcome. My imagination ran wild.

As I made my way across the city to the bus stop on that cold, damp November day I was filled with a mixture of excitement and nerves. I had not asked for extra time off from the office where I was working. How could I say I was attending an interview? And in any case I didn't consider it important, I was so confident that following this interview I would be handing in my notice. Believing that first impressions were important I was anxious to look my best. I wore the little suit I had recently made, the height of fashion at the time and made from the most expensive Jacqmar material, and my newest stilettos. I had long since ditched my specs but I still had a problem with my hair which I knew would suffer in the damp drizzle of the day. The bus stopped outside the headquarters, a large important looking building with a long drive. Double doors let me into a large oak panelled room, the likes of which I had only seen in films, and I approached the reception desk with all the confidence I could muster. I was conscious of the nervousness in my voice as I announced who I was and why I had come. The receptionist glanced through the appointments diary, then asked me to take a seat. A few minutes later she asked my name again then disappeared behind one of the many closed doors leading off this room. This slight delay gave me time to compose myself a little. My confidence was returning and I was beginning to relax for the first time since I had left the office. I wondered what this person would be like. She knew little about me and yet I felt sure the interview would go well and by the time I left the building I would be on the first step to becoming a cookery demonstrator. My day dreaming was all too soon interrupted by the voice of the receptionist saying "I'm very sorry dear but I think there's been a mistake. Mrs Freeman is in Stafford all day at a meeting and there's no record of your appointment in the diary, she must have forgotten about you." The tone of her voice made it sound so trivial a matter. She had no idea the effect her words had on me. I could not speak, my little world had been shattered … until I remembered the office and I knew I must get back before anyone realised I had been absent for so long. I ran like the clappers to the nearest bus stop. I wouldn't be handing in my notice this week after all!

At home it was my Father who first showed any real interest in my cooking. He was a hard-working man and Sunday afternoon was the only time he took off from his business. He would always ask me to "make some of those dainty little sandwiches" for tea and I would spend hours in the freezing cold verandah thinly slicing endless rounds of bread, softening Echo margarine (he would not eat butter or any other brand of margarine), and preparing fillings for his favourite sandwiches, usually from a tin of black market John West salmon.

I remember little of that first examination and have no record of my entries for the practical test, although I do remember it including an elaborate salad arranged on a large flat plate – very different from the one my Mother would have made in a salad bowl with an upturned saucer on the base to catch the water dripping from the lettuce, with lettuce often being the sole ingredient.

I do remember the day of the practical examination. It was a Saturday morning and my Father had reluctantly agreed to leave his shop for a couple of hours to collect me, my completed dishes and all the other paraphernalia needed for the exam. It would have been quite impossible for me to have returned by bus. Sometime later I was told that my Father had proudly shown my entries, laid out in the boot of his car, to all the husbands waiting to collect their wives.

I was unhappy about my theory paper, convinced that I had failed and wouldn't be able to join the remainder of the class for the two year advanced course. Despite the fact that, with the exception of Stella, most of my class mates were old enough to be my Mother, we had built up a really happy relationship and I very much wanted to remain a part of that group. But I needn't have worried, I passed both the practical and the theory examinations and in the September of that year I returned to enrol for the City and Guilds 244 advanced cookery course.

Everything about this course was indeed advanced, to me at any rate. The preparation, cooking and the presentation of all ingredients was far more elaborate than it had been for the elementary course. The advanced kitchen was also different. Shelves displayed an unusual assortment of tins, copper moulds and silver dishes. Modern electric food mixers and liquidizers also formed part of the equipment which we were actually allowed to use for this course. Washing-up ladies were employed so that at the end of a demanding and tiring evening we were not faced with a sink full of used pots and pans – what a bonus that was!

We were introduced to more advanced sauce making – béchamel, velouté, and espagnole. We were shown how to make aspic jelly and how to combine this with béchamel sauce, or mayonnaise, home made of course, to make a chaud-froid sauce. This was a tricky and time consuming task. The correct thickness of the sauce was vitally important and the stirring of the two ingredients over ice until it was of the correct consistency to gently coat the food required great skill. Failure to recognise each of these stages spelt disaster, the sauce would either run straight off the food or smother it (back to the heavy blanket syndrome!), neither resulted in good presentation and both time and ingredients were wasted. With luck and endless patience the most eye catching presentation was possible using this delicate sauce.

The making of hot and cold soufflés, creams and sweet and savoury mousses, also formed part of the syllabus. Here again a combination of patience and skill were necessary to achieve perfect results. When making a mousse a copper mould had first to be lined with sweet or aspic jelly into which delicately cut pieces of ingredients, appropriate to the flavour of the mousse, be it sweet or savoury, were arranged to form a pattern on the base and sides of the mould. This was then set on ice before the prepared mousse was added. Insufficient care taken when running the mould through hot water immediately before it was turned out could result in the decoration left clinging to the mould. Too much hot water could melt the jelly and the mousse was served with the decoration sliding down the sides and with the mousse itself standing in liquid jelly – not an appetising sight for an examiner to witness.

Having perfected the art of lining and decorating the mould, attention then turned to making the mousse filling, the consistency of which was the key to success. If made too runny, the whole mousse, decoration and all, would flop over the serving dish like an overweight jellyfish. Again endless time had been wasted and you were left, like the mousse, feeling somewhat deflated.

The art of making Genoese sponges, a skill I was never able to perfect, was demonstrated, elaborate pastries and tarts were baked and many other advanced recipes were included in this course. I was rarely happier than when I was decorating cakes and gateaux which provided me the opportunity to show off my presentation skills. Every recipe had to be tackled with painstaking care from beginning to end in order to achieve good results and we all soon realised what an important part the basic recipes taught us in the elementary course played in preparing us for these advanced dishes. It had provided us with a sound basic knowledge of cooking, without which we could never have understood and presented these advanced recipes.

My Mother's cooking was basic but adequate. Like most women of her time she did marvellously with the restricted ingredients available. She was a superb pastry maker, a skill my sisters inherited. I have become grateful to the inventor of the food processor which has saved me from endless family criticism of my pastry. I could have listed the contents of my Mothers store cupboard on a postage stamp. The ingredients I was now using were a revelation to me as I suspect they were to some of the others on the course though, unlike me, they never openly admitted it.

Garlic, curry powders and oriental spices, root ginger, asparagus, aubergines and peppers, all very familiar culinary items which will be found in most kitchens today, but forty or so years ago they could only be bought from a few specialist shops. Fortunately most of them were supplied by the college.

I loved every minute of this advanced course and the recipes we made. Well, almost every minute! I clearly remember the evening I spent staring at a chicken and being unable to put my hand inside and draw out its innards. Chickens did not come ready dressed in those days with the giblets conveniently placed in a plastic bag. Fortunately for me Mrs Paxton took pity on me and plunged her naked hand into the carcass of my bird and removed the offending organs. Had she not, I think I might still be standing over that chicken!

Although I never tired of the time I spent experimenting and cooking these advanced recipes, I worried about the advanced theory. As Margery had predicted we received instruction from a visiting dietician. He lectured us for an hour every Monday evening. He taught us, among other things, how to access the amounts of protein, vitamins, minerals and carbohydrates needed for a healthy diet. He illustrated this with the following examples – meat and two veg, fish and chips, bread and cheese. These, he said, were perfectly balanced meals. It was from his lips that I first heard the word 'metabolism' when he talked about the ways in which our bodies converted food into energy. He advised us to think of the food we eat as a repeating pattern of coloured beads. If a colour is missed out, or if too much of one colour is added, the pattern is broken, the diet is unbalanced and the eventual result could well be ill health. I still believe these basic principles are as true now as ever they were. He talked about diabetics and the special diet they needed – this I think was the only diet spoken of at that time. He also regularly set question papers which I read but did not understand and hadn't a hope of answering correctly. I would hand in my paper and leave the room feeling totally inadequate and out of my depth. Would I, I frequently asked myself, ever be able to pass an advanced examination theory paper?

An example of my course notes using shorthand

3

I was now 21 and no nearer to being accepted for training than when I first left school at the age of 15. I began to doubt whether I would ever achieve my ambition to become a cookery demonstrator. I became discontented with my job. My sisters and most of my friends were getting married. Stella had married and was about to join Stanley who had taken a commission in the army and was posted to Germany.

The opportunities for travel were limited. University students hitchhiked in France but that was about it. I wanted to explore other places. I wanted to get away from Birmingham and the Black Country; I longed for a complete change of job and of environment.

The opportunity came sooner than expected. My parents returned from a visit to some friends who had recently retired to Torquay. My Mother, concerned about my obvious unhappiness, confided in her friend who responded by offering to let me stay with them for a short time and if I enjoyed it perhaps I might find a summer job. I needed no persuading; the summer was just beginning and promising to be a good one. Almost before that good lady had time to make up my bed, I was on her doorstep.

I very soon found a job as a receptionist in an hotel, found a bed-sit just around the corner and stayed for two memorable summers. This all took place before hotel winter breaks became so popular and I was fortunate that my hotel was one of the few in Torquay which remained open all year round and my job was secured during the winter months. Even so these winter months were extremely dull. The hotel was only partly occupied by a handful of retired people. There were few young people in Torquay and very little to occupy one's free time. I had become friendly with a receptionist from a nearby hotel and together we enrolled for evening classes at the local college of food. The course was cake decorating and chocolate making and there was no examination at the end!

The teacher was both talented and gentle. She introduced me to many elaborate forms of cake decorating. I also learnt how to crystallize violets and angelica and how to make chocolates. That Christmas each member of the class produced beautifully decorated Christmas cakes and I presented my family and friends with boxes of home made chocolates. I was fascinated by this course, it introduced me to a type of cooking which I had not known before and helped me to develop more culinary skills. Unfortunately I have mislaid many of the recipes I was given but I still enjoy decorating cakes and, over the years, have made many wedding, birthday and other special occasion cakes. Little did I realise that in years to come my kitchen would resemble a chocolate factory each December as I made pounds of chocolates and fudge, some to occupy a large tray which was passed around the table after our family Christmas lunch. The remainder I put into boxes to take to friends and neighbours.

The two summers I spent in Torquay were fun but the prospect of a second winter was far from appealing and I became impatient to move on. The hotel proprietors gave me every Saturday afternoon off and I spent most of these with my newly made friend Yvonne Keck. Yvonne rented the most attractive little cottage in the garden of a big house and most of these afternoons were spent with her, talking, having tea and eating delicious coffee and walnut gateau which I usually bought on my walk up to her cottage. On one such visit towards the end of my second summer, she said, "What are you going to do with yourself? Don't stay in Torquay as I've done. It is too late for me to make the move now. There are so many places to see and things to do. Go to London." Go to London? I was scared at the very sound of it. "I couldn't do that," I said. "What would I do? Where would I live? I only ever remember going to London once as a child when Father took us to a trade show in Earls Court." "That doesn't matter," replied Yvonne. "You could get a job with the BBC, or one of the big oil companies, they often offer accommodation to staff moving into London, you'd soon meet people. You could go to all the shows and the art galleries, there are so many things to do in London, I think everyone should spend a time working and living in London."

On the walk back to my bed-sit I thought about this and

decided it would do no harm just to write to the BBC. I doubted they would have a job to offer me and even if they did I didn't have to take it. I put pen to paper and posted a letter the next day. I was flabbergasted to receive a reply by return of post offering me an interview, all expenses paid. Wow, I thought, they must be keen to meet me! Within a month of that initial conversation over tea and cake, I had packed my bags, left Torquay and arrived one Sunday evening at the BBC Hostel in New Cavendish Street W1. My parents were horrified and my poor Mother was distraught.

Yvonne when I first met her with Peter my nephew and Minky, Yvonne's cat

4

I spent five exciting years in London working at the BBC in sound and television. I did many of the things Yvonne had suggested, and more, in addition to making many friends. Amongst these was Mary Mattock, with whom I shared a room at the hostel, and Ann Graham, who introduced me to the Coffee Pot Club, where I met Anthony Drake Smith (nicknamed Adam Smith), who was soon to become my husband. Adam's parents lived in Harborne, a smart area of Birmingham, and so, as we both had families and many friends in the Midlands we decided to leave London and begin married life in Hagley in Worcestershire. We were soon blessed with two sons, Edward (Ed) and William (Bill), and daughter, Helen (Nell).

Adam had many friends (the 'crowd') from his days at Birmingham University and we often visited them. All the wives of these friends seemed to excel in the art of cooking and entertaining, of which I had done little. I was anxious not to let Adam down but with a mortgage, and a young family, money was scarce and the housekeeping always seemed to feature last on our list of financial priorities. My

Mother's motto had always been, "Waste not, want not" and my Father had taught us, "A penny of your own is worth a pound of anyone else's". Knowing there was no extra money available for the housekeeping purse, I remembered my parents' words of wisdom and decided I must somehow make a little go a long way.

Faced with this challenge I thought back to my cookery course in Birmingham. I resurrected my notes and old course text books and recipes and soon discovered I had managed to retain much of what I had been taught, including some of the theory! The importance of planning a well balanced diet using fresh ingredients of the best quality, the essential preparation of ingredients before they are cooked, and the art of presenting meals beautifully, all these things came flooding back to me. I drew on this knowledge and concentrated on these three important points. I planned and shopped with great care. I took time over the preparation of ingredients. I discovered it was possible to achieve a good balance of flavours even on a small budget. I remembered the importance of 'extracting' flavours and of 'sealing in' flavours before or during cooking so that the meal was really tasty. Because presentation was always so important to me, I took care never to crowd ingredients on to a plate. I was further assisted in the presentation of my recipes by the generosity of my Mother-in-law, herself a good cook. I still remember her wonderful roast dinners. She gave me many lovely family china, glass and silver plates and dishes which she said she no longer had a need for. I used these constantly and often created recipes especially for them. Mother-in-law was clearly fascinated by my kind of cooking and after one of my meals she would say to family or friends, in a very complimentary way, "It's one of her made up meals."

I remembered also the importance of a well stocked store cupboard and fridge in which there could always be found a quantity of jellied stock, a little white sauce, a teaspoon of apple purée or a pot of royal icing. I never threw anything away, unless it was bad of course. I discovered that a leftover teaspoon of sauce or apple purée could add that little extra something to the dish I was concocting. The individual flavours of my meals depended very much on the 'bits' I had in store. I find it sad that most modern cookery books do not emphasise the value of left over bits and how they can be made into réchauffé meals.

I became more adventurous with cooking and planning. I taught myself not to confuse the palate by mixing or presenting too many flavours at one meal. I prepared ingredients in advance so that I had only to assemble them for cooking. I would cook a main course a day or two before it was needed. This 'resting' time gave all the ingredients time to combine resulting in a better blend of flavours and a tastier meal. Furthermore it enabled me to cope with any last minute emergency of which there were many with toddlers in the house. Hopefully I would appear relaxed when our guests arrived, the last thing I wanted was for them to feel their very presence had caused total mayhem.

Always wanting to please our friends, I would make a mental note of their culinary likes and dislikes and these I recorded in a special notebook. This I have mislaid over the years but I remember how it helped me to plan so that I didn't repeat a menu. It was all so important to me.

I also noted how much each meal had cost and I could easily entertain four people serving a three course meal plus coffee and chocolates for as little as £1. I turned entertaining into a game and I challenged myself to provide better meals at reduced cost. Although the cost of living has now increased beyond all recognition, if need be, I can still cater and provide a healthy meal for very little cost.

I also discovered during this early period of entertaining that the test of a good meal lies in its quality and not in its quantity. Guests should never leave a table feeling bloated. After each course they should feel they might just be able to manage a little more, were it offered, but the good hostess knows that to do so would spoil their enjoyment of her meal as a whole. The key to success, I frequently reminded myself was to remember the '3 P's' – Planning – Preparation – Presentation.

The children also became victims of my frugality. Their day started with a teaspoon of Severn Seas Cod Liver Oil and ended with a mug of milky cocoa. As toddlers they were always given a main meal of fresh meat or fish and two vegetables which I minced through a baby mouli and moistened it with water remaining from cooking the vegetables, usually all in one pan. Home made rusks and sponge fingers, jellies made from fresh oranges and lemons, blancmanges and egg custards all formed part of their diet. For tea I often decorated plates of small sandwiches with thin slices of apple, orange segments and black or white grapes, it all helped to tempt their palates and encourage them to try flavours and textures they might otherwise have refused. Gradually I weaned them on to crispy potato scallops, cheesie omelettes and spinach pancakes. Small pieces of cod covered with fresh breadcrumbs and baked with a knob of butter on top were their fish fingers. I taught them how to knead dough and they spent many happy times making bread rolls and plaits and other shapes of their own design. They also enjoyed making dropped scones and we all remember the day Edward wrote 'A Happy Christmas' from dropped scone mixture to the delight of his younger brother and sister.

Party teas would include all their favourite foods – sandwiches shaped like pinwheels, savoury eggs, celery piped with cream cheese, bacon rolled round prunes or mushroom pieces and pinwheels of ham and pate, iced biscuits, petit meringues, macaroons and chocolate swiss roll. A birthday cake might resemble a train, a car, a house, a crinoline lady or a tennis court depending on their age and hobby at the time. Savoury Toad (a variation of Toad in the Hole). Aunty Annie's Cheese Pie and Baked Bean Pie were family weekend favourites.

Ed, who had refused to eat anything other than liver, carrot and potato for lunch for the first two years of his life, still says liver and bacon is one of his favourite meals. Bill enjoys stew and dumplings, and Nell is always happiest if it's roast lamb for Sunday lunch. They were all healthy and I can count on one hand the numbers of days they had away from school through ill health.

The following is an example of my thoughts at that time on planning a healthy diet acceptable to toddlers and young children.

Food for toddlers and young children

Introduce toddlers and young children to new flavours gradually. Present their food in small portions and they will often eat more than if they were given one single large amount. Children are attracted by shapes and colours. Introduce these as often as you can in the form of a garnish. Remember that you are setting their eating pattern for life and the more quickly and easily they accept good wholesome food the more healthy they will become in adult life.

Our wedding day – May 1965

My Father with Edward (L) and William in our
Hagley garden

Adam's Father

Adam's Mother

Nell was just a few months old when Adam returned from the office one evening looking very serious. "I have some bad news, my job is coming to an end". That was quite a shock. We had three small children, a house, a mortgage, no savings and now no job – the prospect was bleak. Vacancies for Chartered Accountants seemed few and far between at that time. After several anxious and difficult months Adam was offered a job based in Stroud, Gloucestershire. This was a great relief but it meant we had to up sticks, leave family and friends and move sixty miles down the motorway. It was the early 1970's and the first of the house market 'gazumping' came into play. House prices were rising so fast that if you sold a house and didn't buy another within a matter of weeks it was almost certain you would have to down grade and settle for whatever you could afford. We were fortunate. Having sold our house quickly, on my first visit to Stroud an estate agent told us of a plot of land which had only that week been purchased by a local builder and plans submitted for a house. This plot was in the middle of the hill village of Bisley. We located the village and the site and I made a note of the name and address of the builder. A few evenings later when Adam was out and I was sewing, my thoughts turned to our future and where we might find a house. I remembered the village where we had seen the plot of land. It seemed a nice village and the land was in a good situation. Across the road was an old vicarage and grounds, and a short walk away was a village pub, an attractive old Cotswold building. I decided to give the builder a ring. When Adam returned home a few hours later I was so excited. "We have a house," I said. "I telephoned and spoke to the builder who was surprised I even knew he had purchased the land." "Yes," he said, "I plan to build a house on the plot, and yes, you can buy it." He lived in a nearby village and the conversation ended with a date being fixed for us to visit him to see the plans and finalise details. We were now able to leave Hagley and while our house was being built we rented a company house opposite the factory, No. 2 Gladfield Villas, which we called The Villa! A few months later we took up residence in Bisley and were soon grateful to the company who had decided they no longer needed Adam's services – what a favour they did us. There was also sadness for us all at this time with the sudden death of my Mother.

During that first summer we had a constant stream of weekend visitors, both family and friends and my Mother-in-law, Granny, often stayed with us for several weeks at a time. It was on one of these early visits that we went fruit picking with the intention of jam making … It was a hot summer's morning and we decided to motor across the river to Newent. Granny and I set out armed with sun hats, drinks and three small children, all very excited at the prospect of this new adventure. It had been my intention to pick strawberries only in the hope that a much needed touch of magic might be added to my attempts at this particular jam. All previous attempts having resulted in strawberry syrup. To our surprise, on arrival at the farm there were strawberries, raspberries, loganberries, gooseberries, red and black currants, all awaiting our eager picking fingers. We all ate and picked, in that order, our silent concentration being interrupted only by the occasional cries of "I've never seen such a big strawberry in my whole life" from Ed, all of six years old.

We started the homeward journey with my little car packed to capacity with baskets of fruit of all kinds, three weary children and an equally exhausted Granny. Stopping at a grocer's shop for ice creams I learnt there was a sudden sugar shortage. "Sugar is likely to become rationed," said the excited shopkeeper. That was all I needed to hear. On arrival home I realised my preserving pan was far too small for the large quantities of fruit we had picked. After much telephoning around the village the Vicar's wife came to my rescue and loaned me her beautiful new, large, preserving pan – which I promptly burnt! It was an unusually hot summer and the picked fruit was deteriorating by the minute in the garage. I had no freezer, and I soon discovered I had precious few empty jam jars. More telephone calls were made and notices placed in the windows of the village shops and post office urgently requesting jam pots of any size. The whole village by now must have been wondering about this mad cook who had arrived in their midst. Between all the telephone calls I had yet another abortive attempt at making strawberry jam and vowed I would never again waste time and ingredients on a luxury which was clearly beyond my ability. Eventually grateful neighbours with freezers shared most of our crop and the remainder we ate and enjoyed and then forgot about, until the next jam season.

One day I read an article in a national newspaper about a lady who was giving cookery demonstrations in her kitchen. This immediately took me back to my school days and I remembered the ambition I had once had to be a cookery demonstrator. Cookery demonstrations in one's own kitchen. It sounded a nice idea. The village in which we were now living would provide the right setting but our house and kitchen were too small to contemplate such a venture. If we ever moved to a larger house perhaps I would think about it more seriously.

All too soon the time arrived for Nell, our youngest child to start school and I found myself wondering what I would do with myself and all this extra time available to me. For ten years my days had been planned around the needs of our three children and our home. Life was going to be very different with all of them at school. As a relative newcomer to the village I had few acquaintances and no real friends. How would I occupy my time? Then I remembered the cookery course I had attended in my late teens. I had always promised myself that one day I would complete the advanced course. With this in mind I decided to write to the College of Food in Cheltenham and make enquiries about possible enrolment in the September of that year.

My letter was answered by a telephone call. I was told the course I had originally started in Birmingham had long since been discontinued but that I would be very welcome to join the new City and Guilds Home Economics course which had replaced it. This, I was informed, was a two year course requiring attendance one day a week. Successful candidates could, if they wished, go on to obtain a teaching diploma which would involve a further two years study. The caller continued to tell me that the present class was into its second term but, because of my previous experience, if I wished, I could join them after the Easter break. The conversation ended with me being invited to go along to meet the group the following week. There were about a dozen ladies on the course of a similar age to myself and I decided to accept the offer to join them. The timing of this course was opportune in many ways. It helped me to adjust to the new stage in the development of the children. It gave me something to think about and to plan for, and it gave me a complete day out each week. This happened at a time when I was experiencing much loneliness and was still missing the companionship of my family and close friends whom I had left behind in the Midlands. The ladies on the course were welcoming and friendly and, like Stella and Marjorie, they have remained good and faithful friends. Over the many years we have shared joys and tragedies and we still meet for lunch at the college restaurant twice a year and talk about the course, husbands, family weddings and, for most, grandchildren.

The course itself soon brought home to me the advantages the ladies on that very first evening course had had over me. With ten years cooking experience under my belt I never had to think what sort of spoon to use to stir the sauce, or whether to use plain or self-raising flour. Providing a well balanced diet had become part of my daily routine, and cooking a roast and two veg. was child's play – including making the gravy! I realised how naïve I must have been all those years ago and I wondered how I had survived even one month of that first course. I also realised how very ordinary my cooking had become and once again I was challenged to be more adventurous with recipes. Drawing on the knowledge I now had I soon began to develop my own style of cooking and, most exciting of all, to create my own recipes.

The course work itself was of a very relaxed nature and following the discipline of my previous City and Guild courses I found this difficult to adjust to especially when the teacher said, "Don't give yourselves too much to do on the day of the practical test, prepare as much as you are able at home." I wondered how the examiner would know whether we had cheated and allowed someone else to prepare our recipes!

But one of the great things I remember was the introduction to the preserving of fruits about which, as part of my examination, I wrote an essay entitled 'Preserves on a Shoestring'. The two ingredients in which I was most interested were the preservation of whole fruits and the crystallizing of orange peel. Over the years my Christmas confections were incomplete if they did not include Pineapple Chocolates made from crystallized pineapple and Chocolate Orange Sticks made from crystallized orange or tangerine peel. The children were instructed by me how to peel oranges so that the peel remained in quarter sized pieces. I stored this in the refrigerator until I had a suitable amount to crystallize. I was slightly amused on one occasion when I overheard Bill instruct his friend how to peel an orange and keep it for Mother. I have often wondered what the friend told his family when he got home!

Edward 5 years   William 3 years

Helen 5 years

6

The end of this three year course, which I was thrilled to pass with distinction, coincided with us moving house. We had not realised how quickly we would outgrow our present house and not wishing to leave the village, we were overjoyed when a house just two doors up the road became available. We learnt about the sale quite by coincidence. We returned from a holiday to find our neighbour's car occupying the drive. This didn't bother us but he came out to apologise and we went on to ask if everything had been all right while we were away. "A strange thing happened yesterday", he said, "I noticed a fellow looking through your windows, I said you were on holiday and could I help, but he had some papers in his hand and was looking for Bear House which he wanted to view with the possibility of buying." Property was really difficult to come by, especially an old Cotswold house with character and I couldn't believe such a property within yards of our house had been sold. I pleaded with my husband to telephone the owner, a widowed lady whom we knew well. The house had not as yet been sold although several people had been to view it. We fixed a time to view it the next morning.

Until that morning I had never even walked through the garden gate but on my very first step into the kitchen of Bear House a familiar feeling came over me, the feeling I had experienced when, as a schoolgirl, I had first entered the prefabricated hut in which I was given my first lesson in cookery. I knew immediately that if we were ever fortunate enough to buy Bear House I would realise my childhood ambition and, like the lady in the newspaper, I would give cookery demonstrations in my kitchen.

We moved to Bear House the following March and I had just a few months to decide whether to continue my studies and go on to take the teaching diploma, or to start my demonstrations. With little hesitation I decided on the demonstrations. Something told me that if I delayed them by two years I would never take the plunge. The time and the circumstances seemed opportune.

I planned my first course of demonstrations to begin on 5th October of that year (1978), and to continue every alternate week with a break during the month of December. My programme up to Christmas included Buffet Cookery; Party Puddings and Gateau; Entertaining on a Budget; Icing and Decorating the Christmas Cake, and Preparing for Christmas. Between January and March of the following year I offered Fish Cookery; Yeast Cookery; Chicken and Game Cookery; Strudel and other Pastries; Soups and Starters.

I decided I could seat 12 in the kitchen and my booking form invited people to arrive for coffee and biscuits at 10.30 am. The demonstration would commence at 11 am. and would last for approximately one and a half hours. I asked a fee of £1.50p per person for each demonstration including coffee and biscuits and I decided to offer for sale all the dishes I had demonstrated for the cost of the ingredients only. I posted my programmes in letter boxes in Bisley and neighbouring villages, and gave them to all my friends. I also advertised in two local newspapers. The response I had was encouraging and within a short time bookings were flooding in.

There was now a lot to think about and much to do. I had to decide what to demonstrate and to prepare recipe sheets. I had to think about the order in which I would demonstrate the chosen dishes, there would be no time to waste. I made detailed time sheets based on the ones I had been taught to make at that first cookery course in Birmingham. Shopping had to be thought about too. This would have to be done with care and only the choicest ingredients could be purchased. I had to choose the right dish or plate on which to present the completed dishes. The preparation seemed endless but I enjoyed it all. Everything had to be worked out to the finest and the last detail if the demonstrations were to run smoothly. I must be confident and relaxed in order to create the right atmosphere for my audience. It was important that they left my kitchen excited by my recipes and eager to try them for themselves. Would I remember all the tips I wanted to pass on? Would I be able to talk and concentrate on cooking all at the same time? Would I find myself speechless? I mentioned this last dilemma to Adam but all he said was, "My dear, whatever else happens, of one thing I am quite certain, you will never be lost for words."

Everything went like clockwork on the morning of that first demonstration. Ingredients were weighed up, coffee was ground and ready to be made, the dining table was set with coffee cups and home made biscuits and I had even found time to light a welcoming fire. I was pleased with my organisation and felt composed and ready to receive my audience. All that remained for me to do was to place the chairs in the kitchen. To my dismay, no matter how much I juggled with them I could not fit twelve chairs into the available space. I hadn't any special chairs, just dining chairs and odd chairs scattered around the house. My initial decision to seat 12 people was based on visual guesswork only – I had looked at the available space beyond my demonstration table and decided there was room for twelve chairs, it never occurred to me to test the space. Furthermore, I had completely overlooked the fact that our dining chairs had widely splayed legs making it impossible to place them as close together as was necessary. At this point my calm turned into panic. However was I going to explain to nearly half my audience, the majority of whom were complete strangers to me, that they would have to stand throughout the demonstration? This totally unexpected hitch triggered all kinds of negative thoughts in my head. Whatever would I do if everything went wrong? What would happen if I burnt everything? If my cakes didn't rise? Would my timing really work or would I keep them here half the afternoon? I had never done a demonstration in my life, why hadn't I had the sense to do a dummy run? These ladies were probably all excellent cooks, what could I teach them they didn't already know? I'd even had the nerve to charge them to watch me cook. I'd done some mad things in my life, but this was quite the maddest. All these thoughts were suddenly interrupted by a ringing in my ears, there was no turning back now, my audience were arriving. In my haste to answer the door I nearly fell over a kitchen stool and there lay the answer to my dilemma – four stools would provide the extra seats needed and the dresser would form a back rest.

As soon as everyone was seated in the kitchen I began by saying "Welcome to Bear House and to this morning's demonstration". This, I had decided, was a nice way to set the scene, and it gave me a few seconds to face my audience en masse, and to compose myself. I remember very little about that first demonstration other than, at the end, I covered my worktable with a pretty cloth on to which I placed an arrangement of flowers before displaying all the dishes I had demonstrated. I concluded by thanking my audience for attending. I hoped they had enjoyed my demonstration and that I had introduced them to some new recipes and given them some new ideas. They responded with an enthusiastic round of applause and proceeded to make bookings for the remainder of the course.

Exhausted, I reflected on the morning and was pleased with the way that first demonstration had gone. My audience had clearly enjoyed it and so had I. From the moment I had started I was never nervous – or speechless! Demonstrating my recipes was theatre to me and I loved every minute of it. But there was a long way to go. Before my next demonstration in two week's time, Nora, Adam's aunt, was coming to stay with us, and then the builders were moving in!

Whereas my Mother-in-law was a good cook, her sister Nora, (one of the six Drake sisters), who preferred to be called Ra, was an excellent cook and a perfect hostess and taught me a lot. At eighteen she had been presented at Court (a Debutante), and married Lesley Forbes, a young airforce officer. They spent the war years in Iraq and the Middle East. They had done everything "from the front row," as Ra often told me. On retirement they moved to Chute in Hampshire from where Lesley set up a mill and they were one of the first producers of stone ground wholemeal flour. This they parcelled up and posted to addresses countrywide. On Lesley's death Ra sold out to one of the flour mill companies and moved to Pont Street, London for a few years before moving to Buckinghamshire. We all have many happy memories of summer parties at her lovely cottage in Little Chalfont, often when Aunty Margaret (another of the Drake sisters), her son Philippe, his wife Bénédicte and their son Dominique were over from Belgium. The food was always superb, and plentiful, to the delight of the children whose eyes nearly popped at the sight of the wonderful chocolate cakes and huge bowls of fresh peaches (when I might buy two to share between five). I grew very fond of Ra, although in the early days I found her a formidable character, quite frightening, but I learnt to hold my own, as on the occasion when she taught me to eat artichokes. Adam and I had been invited to a mid week luncheon. Also there were Peter, one of Adam's many cousins on the Drake side, and his lovely Norwegian wife, Evy. Nora's dining table was perfection as always – crisply laundered white napkins, polished silver, sparkling crystal and a lovely arrangement of garden flowers. At each place setting was our first course, an artichoke. I was placed to the right of Ra. She passed me the vinaigrette which I immediately spooned over my artichoke only to notice everyone else spooned it around theirs. Adam had taught me that you should always wait for your hostess to begin to eat and I waited for Ra to begin, but she didn't, nobody did, and suddenly I felt all eyes were centred on me. I looked up at Ra who said, "Well, begin," to which I replied, "I don't know how to," as well she knew from the moment I had applied the vinaigrette to my artichoke. I was then given a lesson on how to prepare and eat an artichoke. The lesson was interesting but I found the eating of the artichoke a disappointing experience and one which I have not repeated.

My original plan had been to hold my demonstrations fortnightly, leaving the week in between for me to practise

A.

COOKERY DEMONSTRATIONS AT BEAR HOUSE

1978   5 October   : Buffet cookery (including a starter, main course and pudding)

       19 October   : Party puddings and gateaux

       2 November   : Entertaining on a budget

       16 November   : Icing and decorating the Christmas Cake

       30 November   : Preparing for Christmas

1979   18 January   : Fish cookery

       1 February   : Yeast cookery.

       15 February   : Chicken and game cookery

       1 March   : Strudel and other pastries

       15 March   : Soups and starters

              .....oOo.....

Coffee is served from 10.15 a.m. and demonstrations commence at 11.00 a.m. prompt and last for approximately two hours.

Recipe sheets are on sale.

All dishes demonstrated are on sale.

Evening demonstrations for parties of twelve or more can be arranged.

FEES : £1.50 per demonstration, payable on booking, and cannot be refunded unless a substitute can be found.

In addition light lunches can be arranged for parties of twelve or more.

From Mo Smith, Bear House, Bisley,

My first Demonstration
programme

1978/9   A.

1. Buffet Cookery.

   Crepes
   Chicken liver pâté
   Savoury loaf (bread).
   Mackerel pâté
   Ham pinwheels.
   Praline meringue.
   Praline powder.

2. Party puddings & gateaux

   Chocolate gateau (genoise cake)
   Sylla Bella
   French fruit flan (open).
   Petit meringues.
   Almond biscuits.

Recipes for my
Demonstrations

57

some recipes. But it didn't work out quite like that and during those first few months there were many unforeseen hitches.

Taking a close look at the kitchen I had decided it would need more than just a new coat of paint before it could be opened to the public – in today's terms, it needed a make-over. With the planned bi-weekly demonstrations, how was this going to happen? The kitchen units I had ordered took longer to come than promised and for my first demonstration the kitchen was more or less as it had been when we moved into Bear House just a few months earlier. The white Belfast sink was mounted on bricks, leaving room for a bucket underneath – just like the one in our council house. Although in years to come these became highly priced kitchen status symbols, they were not so at the time and most were being put in the garden and filled with summer flowers, or sent to the scrap heap. The hand-made painted wooden units, although adequate, were looking a little worse for wear and old fashioned – they didn't stand a chance of remaining. Everyone, myself included, craved the latest formica kitchen. We had no kitchen table and I used one we had bought, along with as many other items of furniture I could possibly squeeze into our Mini, from a junkyard I had spied while we were on honeymoon in Scotland. To make it more presentable I covered the somewhat crude, badly painted top with fablon of a wood grain design and hoped the rickety legs would go unnoticed.

I contacted Alan Smith, the builder who had built our previous house and somehow managed to persuade him to agree that he, his carpenter, plumber and electrician would work on my kitchen every other week. I did some-times wonder how, or if it would work out. Bear House is very old, not one wall is straight, and there are lots of nooks and crannies. Painstaking work might be needed to fit the new kitchen in place. Would Alan and his team complete a job and leave my kitchen in a reasonable state for my demonstration the following week? It was essential I had the kitchen to myself for a few days to be able to prepare for the next demonstration. Friends thought I was quite out of my mind. Builders are not the most reliable of people, I was told. You send them away and you'll not see them again for weeks. Would Alan remember our agree-ment? Needless to say they did have many problems but their experience and patience enabled them to tackle and solve each difficulty as it arose. The builder's word was his bond, he kept his promise, for which I was sincerely grateful.

All this activity in the kitchen gave my audience some-thing extra to look forward to. Many had decided to book for the complete course of ten demonstrations and between October and December they saw the kitchen transformed. First came the new sink and units. Then a lovely new work table appeared, replacing the junk yard model. Another week a new floor was laid. Spotlights were fitted another week, new curtains and a matching blind was hung at the door. Smart, comfortable, padded chairs arrived and finally, and for me the most exciting addition of all, a brand new four oven gas fired Aga was installed. My Father had died just before our move to Bear House and I decided the best present I could give myself with the money he had left me was an Aga. It would welcome everyone into the kitchen with warmth and comfort and be a constant reminder to me of a very dear Father who, having been brought up on a farm with meals cooked by his Mother on an old fashioned range, would very much have approved of this, and would have loved Bear House.

I had never cooked on an Aga (what I call 'the cooker without knobs on') and had just a few days to practise and get used to it before my next demonstration. Looking back I have often wondered how people reacted as they walked into my kitchen and saw the only cooker I had was an Aga. I never advertised my demonstrations as Aga cooking and of course always gave conventional oven settings in the recipe sheets. Word got around and lots of people with, or wanting an Aga came to see me cook. They would leave my kitchen deciding to cancel the 2-oven and order a 4-oven model, and many left determined to make room for one. Although Aga now has shops countrywide and, to my knowledge outlets in Europe and America and with teams of specially trained demonstrators, I believe I was the first person to demonstrate Aga cooking in a domestic kitchen.

When twelve ladies were seated my kitchen seemed small and intimate. The first row of three chairs was within inches of my worktable and I was unable to hide any mistakes. But these ladies were clearly enjoying their mornings and the atmosphere was relaxed and informal. They watched my every move, they observed the way I handled and presented ingredients and noted the useful tips I passed on to them, these were based on what I had been taught at my first cookery course in Birmingham Gradually they began to realise the importance of the '3 P's' to which I constantly referred and which to me are the key to successful cooking – Planning, Preparation, Presentation. To explain more fully I suggested that meals be 'planned' to suit the palates of those you are feeding, to fit in with your way of life, to suit your purse and your capability. Shop with care buying only the best quality ingredients, the flavours, colours and textures of which will complement each other. Do not confuse the palate by presenting too many flavours on a plate. 'Prepare' all ingredients with care before they are cooked in order to extract the best flavour and to ensure they are easy to handle, to serve and to digest – there is little more devastating to a cook to find that ingredients are left uneaten. 'Presentation' has always been vitally important to me. If a meal does not look appetising no-one will want to try it. Avoid overcrowding ingredients on to too small a dish or plate. Choose a dish or plate to 'fit' the meal. Garnish or decorate with care and always remember presentation does not have to be elaborate, in fact the simplest presentation is often the most eye catching.

Gradually my audience became less shy. They began to ask questions and to relate their own experiences when following my recipes in their own kitchens. I remember Tatti, a petite Indonesian lady, newly married and newly arrived in England and the Cotswolds. Although she had difficulty speaking and understanding our language, she had no difficulty making the croissants I had demonstrated and was selling them on a regular basis to a coffee shop in Cirencester. There was the lady who attended a dinner party at which the menu was identical to the one she had seen me demonstrate that very morning. There was the young bride who had attempted to impress her in-laws by making an apple strudel. "Don't mention strudel pastry to me again" she laughed, "I got into such a mess that I threw the whole lot, cloth and all, into the bin." And there was the lady who forgot to count the crepes before filling them and to her embarrassment saw one of her guests struggling with a piece of greaseproof paper during an important business dinner party. But the mistakes were not always on the part of my audience. I well remember the morning I attempted to demonstrate the making of puff pastry – having become a Lazy Cook I no longer make or even roll it, but buy it already prepared for use! I began by telling my audience, with all the confidence in the world, that the secret of making puff pastry lay in the correct consistency of the dough before the butter is worked in. "Experience has taught me," I said, "that to each ounce of plain flour a tablespoon of water is needed." I was using eight ounces of flour and I added eight tablespoons of water, counting aloud as I did so. I then proceeded to mix the ingredients together and to my absolute horror the dough, instead of being of a manageable, pliable consistency, was soft and runny and quite unrollable. An unfamiliar silence came over the kitchen and at that moment all I wished was that the floor would open and swallow me up. In my mind I was sure I had not weighed the flour incorrectly. "I must have added too many spoons of water" was my explanation. "No," came the instant reply, "we counted with you." I looked at the glue-like substance in the bowl not knowing what to do. I was confused but also annoyed at messing up this particular pastry which I had really looked forward to demonstrating. Whatever could have gone wrong? The seconds on the kitchen clock ticked by, then the silence was suddenly broken by an observant member of my audience. "Your tablespoon looks much larger than mine" she said. That was where I had made my mistake. When checking over my equipment before the demonstration I had looked at the tablespoons I always used when cooking and decided that, with their missing handles, they were too old and shabby to use at a demonstration and I replaced them with my Mother-in-law's silver serving spoons, not noticing at the time that these were half as big again as my old but familiar tablespoons. I had added the equivalent of 12 tablespoons and not the desired eight. "That," I openly admitted, "will teach me not to show off with the best family silver." But my audience was always pleased when something went wrong, "it gives us confidence," they said. It taught me not to be over-confident. It was one thing to be successful when cooking for family and friends in the privacy of my own kitchen but to demonstrate my recipes in front of an audience with equal success demanded a totally different skill and much concentration.

There was another celebrated occasion for me when the whole village was suddenly plunged into darkness. This happened well before my demonstration was due to begin and I was confident it would return by 11 am. Even if it did not my Aga was not affected by power cuts and I could, if necessary, place candles around the kitchen. It did not occur to me, until I was actually escorting the audience into the kitchen, that I would be unable to use any electrical appliances. That particular demonstration involved much chopping and whisking of ingredients and I warned my audience that they might be here for a very long time, adding, optimistically, that I felt sure the electricity would return any minute. At 12.45 pm. just as my demonstration was ending the lights came on. It surprised us all that despite the preparation having to be done by hand the demonstration had only lasted a few minutes longer than planned. It also endorsed my theory that the two most important items of kitchen equipment needed are a sharp knife and a good chopping board.

Shopping for ingredients could also be a problem. Produce which had been in the shops for months would suddenly disappear the day I needed to buy it. Not believing my eyes I would enquire, "Have you any avocados?" "No, me dear we haven't" would come the reply. "We had some yesterday and they're on order for tomorrow, I don't know why we haven't any today." It was all so unimportant to the assistant. Little did she realise my reputation depended on getting that particular ingredient today!

At the end of that first session I was pleased with the progress I had made. Bookings had been good and there were times when I arranged repeat demonstrations in order to satisfy the demand. People came from all over the county and, occasionally, from overseas. With the exception of a few hiccoughs which I had somehow managed to overcome, everything had gone more smoothly than I could ever have imagined. The atmosphere had been good, the customers were happy and the rewards where often of an unexpected nature like the time when, someone having undergone a kidney transplant said to me,

"Coming to your cookery demonstrations helped me to start living again, I am so grateful to you."

I only demonstrated my own recipes and it gave me great encouragement when often someone would say, "I made that recipe and it worked, it looked just like your's, and everybody loved it." Annie Stevens who latterly washed up and kept everything clear behind the scenes often remarked, "I just love looking at their faces while you are demonstrating, their concentration and their delight when you garnish or decorate something special – I always wish I had a camera." At last I was realising my childhood ambition to be a cookery demonstrator. At this time there were few cookery programmes on television, it was before Delia, and the profession of a chef was not revered as it is today. I was one of only two or three people across the country opening my kitchen to demonstrate my cooking skills, it was quite a unique achievement.

Encouraged by this success I decided to extend my programme for future courses by offering two mornings every alternate week. I also decided to prefix my programme with a little information about myself and about my cooking – the following are examples of these –

A little information about Mo Smith

My interest in cooking began at a very early age and was further developed after my first school cookery lesson at the age of 11. Over the years my enthusiasm for cooking led me to attend many courses at elementary and advanced levels in cookery, cake decorating, chocolate making and home economics resulting in passes with distinction.

65

It is with this background knowledge and many hours of practice that I started my demonstrations at Bear House a year ago. I have developed my own style of cooking and the dishes I demonstrate are my own creation and the methods, the preparation of food of many kinds, and my presentation are unique to me.

My approach to cooking is that it is a craft which, with the correct equipment and a little enthusiasm, can be successfully carried out by everyone resulting in a lot of fun and the satisfaction of serving good home cooked meals. It is in this atmosphere that my demonstrations take place. If you wish to increase your knowledge and add to your repertoire you will, I feel sure, enjoy a relaxed morning in the characterful setting of my Cotswold kitchen. I look forward to having the opportunity of welcoming you and your friends to Bear House and introducing you to 'my kind of cooking'.

My kind of cooking

My kind of cooking is that which does not involve too much time and effort to prepare but which can be presented simply, or in style, depending on the time, the ingredients and, of course the occasion. The ingredients I use are traditional and many of them come from a well stocked store cupboard. If you would like to learn how to get enjoyment from preparing as much as from eating a meal, you will benefit from the demonstrations I give.

Simply Delicious

I have learned from experience that the most successful meals are those which are simple in preparation and content but eye-catching in presentation. They put little strain on personal *resources leaving the cook free to enjoy the company of family and friends. For this reason I have chosen the theme 'simply delicious' for my course of cooking demonstrations at Bear House this winter.*

Needless to say, as with all things which appear simple, skill and dedication are needed to achieve success. The correct preparation and careful cooking of all ingredients is vital, the blending of flavours, colours and textures are important and good presentation is essential. It is this skill that I demonstrate at Bear House where the atmosphere is relaxed and informal. Coffee and biscuits are served before each demonstration providing me with the opportunity of meeting you and introducing you personally to everyone before we go into the kitchen.

Summer cooking

I have planned these demonstrations to help you spend as little time as possible in the kitchen during the summer months. I have created my recipes around the fresh flavours of summer. Let me help you to plan, prepare and present ingredients simply but with the touch of magic summer brings. Practical tips on storing and keeping ingredients fresh will also be given.

I look forward to the opportunity of welcoming you and your friends to Bear House and demonstrating my recipes to you.

Nora's cottage

A group of ladies at my Demonstration

7

I very much enjoyed my first attempts at writing about cookery. How nice it would be to write about cooking in a newspaper or a magazine – something to think about for the future perhaps.

I had never considered these demonstrations in terms of financial reward – no, it was just something I could do from home, it gave me the opportunity to develop the passion I had for cooking and to pass on my skills to others, that was how I thought of it. The fees covered the cost of all ingredients and printing of recipe sheets. Any thoughts I had of making money took away all the enjoyment. Even so, the seemingly endless hours of work involved in preparation were the same whether I was demonstrating to 12 or to 112 people as was brought home to me whenever I was asked to arrange a charity demonstration. And there were other expenses on the horizon. I realised that I could not forever depend on word of mouth recommendations or on people returning year after year, I needed to advertise to get new interest, to keep my name in front of the public and to spread it further afield. I had been fortunate in the early days to be featured in most of the local newspapers, *Stroud News and Journal*, *Wiltshire Standard*, *Gloucestershire Citizen*, *Cheltenham Echo*, but these were bonuses which I couldn't expect to be repeated and in any case they were one-off features which are soon forgotten by the general public. I somehow had to find another way of spreading my name and keeping it constantly in the public eye.

One evening I mentioned this to a friend I met at a drinks party in the village. He advised that I get in touch with Severn Sound, the new local radio station in Gloucester, "They're crying out for people like you," were his parting words. As soon as I got home, out came the portable typewriter on to the kitchen table and I tapped out a letter to the Managing Director of this first local commercial radio station in the area. I cannot recall much about the content of the letter and maybe it was the glasses of wine which gave me the courage to write it. What I do very clearly remember was suggesting that a cookery spot might go down well with their listeners and that I would be the ideal person to do it! A few evenings later the telephone rang and the voice at the other end said, "Hello, is that Mo Smith? It's Christopher Musk here from the new Severn Sound Radio Station. You've written to us about doing a cookery programme. You obviously don't listen to us very often because we already have a cookery spot, it goes out live every other Thursday morning and I've got a couple of ladies who do it." No longer under the influence of alcohol I was thankful this Mr. Musk could not see my embarrassment as I attempted to apologise. I dared not tell him I didn't have a wireless modern enough to pick up their airwaves! "Don't worry," he interrupted, what you're doing sounds quite interesting and original so you can come in one morning and tell the listeners all about it." A date was fixed and Mr. Musk ended the conversation by saying, "Bring a recipe in, the listeners like to send in for them, oh, and a sample of your cooking, and by the way we don't pay you, bye." I replaced the telephone receiver not knowing whether to feel crushed or elated. The family, realising it was no ordinary telephone call came into the kitchen and bombarded me with questions.

I remember that first morning at the radio station very well. Believing first impressions were important, I wore a new pale blue summer skirt and a favourite blouse of the most delicate colours which I had made from a Christian Dior dress handed down to me by 92 year old Francie. Christopher Musk wore loud checked trousers and a t-shirt many sizes too big for him at a time when t-shirts were worn hugging the body and trousers were plain and conservative. He greeted me with a broad smile and a twinkle in his eye and I was immediately put at my ease. I can only describe the studio as bedlam and a far cry from the quiet, sedate studios I had worked in at the BBC. There were lights flashing everywhere, loud music was playing, the telephone was ringing and Christopher suddenly screaming with delight at the sight of the savoury choux I had risen at the crack of dawn to make for him.

There was no rehearsal and everything was live. I was placed in front of a microphone and Christopher, now in a quiet, more serious voice said to me, "At the end of this jingle we will be on the air. I shall introduce you and we'll take it from there, o.k.?" He then continued, "from time to time I shall interrupt you to play requests from listeners, or an advert, so be ready to finish a sentence when I give you the wind down signal otherwise I'll have to cut you off mid sentence which isn't good." During my five years with the BBC in London I had worked in many live studios so the demands and atmosphere of a live studio were familiar to me though I had never actually spoken on the air. But I knew my subject and I was determined not to be nervous. I had taken pages of notes with me but never once referred to them – there just wasn't time, or need. At the end of my 15 minute spot, during which time a listener had phoned in to ask how to prepare pineapple, I was thanked by Christopher for coming in and congratulated on my performance. I was almost tempted to ask if I could come in again but my better judgment told me to wait. A rejection would only spoil the elation that morning had given me. I decided instead to telephone a week or two later which I did, but to no avail. I was reminded of the two regular contributors they already had and the list of visiting contributors was full for the months ahead. But I didn't give up easily and when I telephoned several months later the reply was, "Oh yes, Mo Smith, I've been meaning to telephone you. I'm changing the style of the Food for Thought spot and you're just the person I'm looking for to give it new life. Could you come in every other Thursday morning? I'll leave you to sort out the programme content. You'll be on the air between 10.30 am. and 11 am. with music and adverts every few minutes. Bring some recipe sheets in and some samples of your cooking if you can. We don't pay you I'm afraid and you can't park here but there's an NCP up the road and you can claim your parking fee. Look forward to seeing you, bye." I couldn't believe my luck!

These programmes presented me with a new challenge and I loved doing them. During each programme I gave two or three recipes with useful hints about the preparation. I talked about seasonal fruits and vegetables as they came into the shops and recommended ways of using them. I gave tips about the use of leftover foods, I gave hints on planning parties for Christmas and for children, and I frequently answered telephone calls as they came in whilst we were on air.

I also interviewed visiting speakers, representatives from the farming community and from food manufacturers, and on one occasion I interviewed the well known and at that time celebrity TV cook, Rabbi Lionel Blue. The Rabbi was visiting the West Country with his agent to promote his latest cookery book 'Kitchen Blues'. They were expected at the studio shortly after my programme and Christopher asked me if I would like to stay behind and meet them. As I waited in the reception area Christopher handed me a copy of the book, "Have a look through this," he said. "Think up a few questions you might like to ask, in fact you can do the interview if you like, you know more about cooking than I do. It's a recording so we can always stop the tape and do plenty of editing." Almost before I had time to open the book the Rabbi and his agent arrived and into the recording studio we went. I was fortunate to be interviewing such a relaxed and humorous celebrity and the interview was recorded without any stops, and needed no editing. I was congratulated by the Rabbi, his agent and

Christopher. Then the Rabbi said "You clearly know a lot about cooking, what else to you do?" I told him about my demonstrations and said that one day I would like to write a book. "Oh that's easy" said the Rabbi. "All you have to do is pick up a plastic bag from the supermarket, discipline yourself to write ten recipes a day and pop them into the bag, at the end of a month you have a book." He also asked if he could include one of my recipes in the Jewish weekly he contributed to. He presented me with a copy of his book in which he wrote 'To Mo, in memory of a good conversation' and signed, Lionel Blue. I was really thrilled to have been given this opportunity and still have the book and a copy of the tape. Before leaving the studio the agent handed me a sheet of Dorling Kindersley headed paper on to which he wrote his name and said, "If you ever decide to write a cookery book, please get in touch with me."

I loved the buzz and the excitement of broadcasting, although there were times when it went a little too crazy. Such an occasion was when we ran a competition in conjunction with the gas board, the prize being a new cooker. It was decided this cooker be presented at a special Easter Sunday lunch programme to be broadcast from the Cheltenham Town Hall where the ever popular Spring Festival would be taking place. I was to cook a meal in front of the festival audience while Christopher interviewed the winner and members of his or her family. From time to time he was to refer to me for a progress report on the lunch and as I cooked each course I was to serve it to Christopher and his guests who would then make comments. All this was to be broadcast live.

I arrived early on that Easter Sunday morning to find the Town Hall packed with people and stalls. We were to broadcast from one of the side rooms and on entering I was surprised to find the only items on the stage were a ancient cooker and an oval table on which sat a sad arrangement of flowers. None of the other items I had requested and had been promised were apparent. Fortunately I had taken my own pots and pans and all other equipment necessary to cook the meal.

On my way through the main hall to the kitchen I picked one or two choice blooms from the lovely arrangements adorning the main stage in the hope that I might put new life into the wilting arrangement I had been left. Most of the cupboards in the kitchens were locked but, with the help of an assistant, we managed to find enough china and cutlery to enable me to set the table as planned. I had given a lot of thought to the presentation of this meal and I wanted the table to look festive and pretty. Somewhere amongst my many boxes was one of my Mother-in-law's beautifully crocheted white tablecloths, some yellow serviettes and candles and some Easter bonnets I had made, one for each place setting. I got no further than spreading the cloth when a man dressed in black tie and tails appeared. "You can't do that" he said, "I'm doing my show here." Before I could say Jack Robinson my table was pushed to one side and with the help of an assistant the dressed up man set up his props. Excited children suddenly filled the room and the conjuror's act began. He was due to finish at 12.30 pm. I was told. That would give me half an hour to set the table and sort out the ingredients for the meal, I decided that was plenty of time and headed in the direction of the coffee bar. Christopher had not yet appeared.

It was nearly 12.30 pm. when I returned to find the conjurer in full swing. I managed to attract his attention and pointed to my watch but coloured handkerchiefs and white rabbits continued to appear from nowhere, the children were wild with excitement and the conjurer, receptive to their screaming demands, continued unperturbed. At 12.45 pm. the noise stopped, the conjurer had finished at last and the excited children disappeared as quickly as they had arrived. I hastily made my way to the stage, there was no time to waste if I was to be ready before Christopher and his guests arrived. But my efforts were thwarted again, by the conjurer. "You can't work here," he said. "There's a great big hole under the carpet, some of the floor boards are missing, I've nearly broken my neck." The atmosphere of magic was still in the air, and fortunately for me, from nowhere appeared two carpenters. By some miracle by five minutes to one my table was set, the floor had been repaired, sound levels had been taken and in walked Christopher, noisy and effervescent as ever. My improved flower arrangement was immediately replaced by a microphone stand and my beautifully set table was covered with clip. boards, papers, headphones and all the equipment necessary for an outside broadcast. Within seconds we were on air.

Several hours later I drove home feeling physically and mentally exhausted. I could think of better ways of spending an Easter Sunday. I told myself things could only get better, and they did. I was asked to compile a shopping basket to be included in my fortnightly programme, I was invited to park my car in the minute studio parking area and I became the only contributor to be paid a fee, about which I had to keep very quiet!

My voice was now often recognised when I was shopping and I received many telephone calls from listeners asking my advice on cooking. I was invited to open fêtes, to judge produce at local shows and to give talks to local groups. I also arranged demonstrations outside my kitchen for fund raising purposes. My name and my voice were now familiar to many people in Gloucestershire. I enjoyed it all and wanted to do more. "It's all a question of luck, knowing the right people, being in the right place at the right time" said my friend Lilian Foulkes. "Have you updated your CV recently?" I looked at her aghast, I didn't even know what a CV was! Looking back, I suppose I should at this time have thought of getting an agent, but only actors and actresses had agents I said to myself. Thinking things over I decided to be satisfied for the present. After all I had more than achieved my childhood ambition to be a cookery demonstrator, I was now a broadcaster with my own live show. Some might consider that slow progress over three years but perhaps it was as much as I could cope with for the time being. In addition to my demonstrations and broadcasting I had a husband, three children and a house to run!

My portable
typewriter

My first photograph in a local newspaper

An Easter display – Humpty-Dumpty cake, Simnel cake,
Easter bonnets

One day I received an unexpected telephone call from the editor of the county magazine, *Gloucestershire and Avon Life* in which I had once been featured and where I sometimes advertised my demonstrations. A feature was being researched on kitchens and would I be prepared to say what were my favourite items of kitchen equipment and to agree to these and my name being published? I was so taken aback by this sudden interest and before the conversation ended I heard myself asking if the magazine would consider a regular cookery column from me. "It's a nice idea" said the editor, "but we already have a column. Leave it with me to think about and I might get back to you sometime." After several months silence, I took courage and telephoned the editor reminding him of our conversation. He still thought it a nice idea but reminded me of the column they already featured and had done for many years, for the time being it was a non-starter.

Quite by chance one day I met a writer friend in the village. He was interested to hear how my cooking venture was progressing and I told him of my latest attempts to get into writing concluding that, like most magazines, they already had an established cookery column. "Don't be put off by that" said my friend, "just suggest that they extend the cookery page to include a piece from you." What a brilliant idea, why had I not thought of this myself? I went straight home, out came the portable typewriter on to the kitchen table and I very carefully compiled a letter to the magazine editor. I hesitated before opening the reply, I was sure it would be yet another rejection, but I was wrong. A few weeks later the editor talked to me across my kitchen table. "I would like to feature your first column in April. Now, let me think, what do we eat at that time of year? Lamb, yes, spring lamb would be a good choice for your first piece. I would like 1,000 to 1,500 words on lamb." That editor had no idea of the effect his request had on me. My mind went into complete turmoil and panic set in. What have I done? How could I possibly write a cookery column, when I knew so little about grammar or punctuation? As a child I couldn't even speak the Queen's English, how was I now going to write a column for a magazine? What a mad thing I had done by suggesting it. What a crazy situation I have got myself into. And what do I know about lamb? How can I possibly write 1,500 words about it? Why do I always act on impulse, why don't I give myself time to think about things, will I never learn? As these and other muddled thoughts reeled around in my head I heard the editor say, "And for each copy we will pay you £15" – somehow that only made my situation even worse!

I thought very carefully before starting that first copy. How was I going to make my column different? How was

I going to hold the interest of the readers and make them want to try my recipes and look forward to my next column? I had somehow to establish my own particular style. I was by now well practised in talking about cooking, could I put my words on paper? Eventually I decided to write my column as a story leading into my recipes and the only difficulty I can remember was keeping it to a minimum of 1,500 words!

Seeing my name, photograph and words in print for the very first time was quite a shock. Receiving my first cheque was a tremendous thrill. This, together with the fee I was now paid for my broadcasts brought my regular monthly earnings up to £40 – I felt like a millionaire and decided it was time perhaps to write a CV.

Cooking had now become a way of life and every day presented me with a different challenge. One day I could be writing my column for the magazine, another I might be decorating a wedding or special occasion cake. In complete contrast another day my time could be spent preparing for a demonstration or shopping for new items for my shopping basket which had now become a regular feature of my broadcasts. In addition a lot of my time was spent experimenting with ingredients and flavours and creating new recipes. Because I used my own recipes only, I now needed an average of twenty new recipes a month. As you can imagine food was never far from my mind.

I became the area selling agent for Magimix, the new food processor being introduced into this country which, at that time, could only be purchased through a few specialist

Mo Smith

Bear House
Bisley
Stroud
Gloucestershire

Gloucester 770298

CURRICULUM VITAE

Cookery Demonstrator

Cookery demonstrations given at Bear House since 1979

A cookery demonstration at Cheltenham Town Hall finalising a competition set and judged by Mo Smith for Severn Sound Radio and the South West Gas Board. This demonstration was broadcast live.

Charity demonstrations:

A local handicapped school

The arthritics Society.

The N.S.P.C.C. - this demonstration is planned for the 3rd August at The Crest Hotel, Gloucester. Jilly Cooper will be present and will present the raffle prizes.

Broadcasting

Severn Sound Radio - since 1982 a programme each fortnight broadcast live between 10.15 and 11.00a.m. This includes details of the weekly shopping basket, supplying and discussing recipes and providing a recipe sheet which listeners may send for. Conducting interviews with guest speakers, e.g. representatives from Anchor Foods Ltd., The British Meat and Livestock Comm. and the British Cheese Council.

Promoting and judging competitions over the air.

Inserts into other programmes.

Representing Severn Sound at outside cookery events e.g. Demonstration by the Meat and Livestock Commission, The Sunday Times Cookery Roadshow.

Journalism

Gloucestershire and Avon Life Magazine - since 1983 a monthly cookery column with photograph

Gloucester "What's On" magazine - a monthly recipe and photograph.

Recipes and articles in local newspapers.

Local celebrity

Judging and opening local fetes.

Giving talks to clubs and societies about how my interest in cooking began as a child.

My first CV

shops and agents such as myself. I am reminded here of a lovely story. I was giving a Magimix demonstration in our village W.I. Hall during which I said something like – "cooking is a craft and like any other craft the right tool for the right job is important." A member of the audience was married to a carpenter and she related my remark to her husband. The next morning there was a cheque on the table for her to buy a Magimix! I was contacted by the Aga company and invited to attend their demonstrator seminars. This gave me an insight into the manufacture of the Aga and kept me up to date with new developments. My days were long and busy and I felt extremely privileged, I was working at my hobby, an opportunity few people have the good fortune to enjoy, I felt fulfilled and content.

Amongst all these activities, the one which often gave me greatest pleasure and the opportunity to use my creative skills, was when making and decorating wedding, special occasion or Christmas cakes. I could lose myself for hours while shaping roses and petals by hand using royal icing. An added bonus was that Doris Fear, our dear friend and neighbour who lived to be 100 years old and who Adam affectionately called a 'centipede', loved to come and sit at the kitchen table and watch me ice and decorate cakes. Her company was, as always, a great joy to both Adam and myself.

Many of these creations had quite a story attached to them about which I often wrote in my *Gloucestershire and Avon* column. The following are two examples ending with, Belle, our lovely golden retriever taking part in the celebration! –

Christmas Goodies

December is a month when we often feel stretched to the limit. Cooking apart, there are many extra demands on our time and energy. Writing cards, decorating the tree, attending endless nativity plays and carol services and extra shopping expeditions for those vital last minute presents. It was during such an outing a couple of years ago that I saw the most wonderful gingerbread house. Completely carried away by its splendour I decided I had to copy it and drew a rough sketch on my shopping list. My family were too grown up for such a fairytale creation but I decided I could make it for Liz and Pete's young family who we were visiting on Boxing day.

I pride myself on being the sort of person who works best under pressure and repeatedly say "I can catch up tomorrow". I never do, but just to utter these words in a carefree way injects a necessary calmness into my system. But with literally a handful of days left to Christmas, was I pushing myself too far this time?

Determined not to fail, once home I lost no time making paper templates. Working well into the early hours and using many batches if ginger biscuit paste I shaped and baked the walls and roof of the house. It took the whole of the next day to stick them all together then they were left in the kitchen overnight to dry. Somehow time was allotted on Christmas Eve to decorate the sides and the roof which I piped with literally pounds of royale icing to resemble deep snow. Finally, liquorice allsorts were dotted over the roof, a Father Christmas stuck in the chimney and the house was complete. I was really thrilled with my achievement and could hardly wait to present it to Sarah and Robert. Meanwhile it was displayed on a table well out of reach of Belle our golden retriever!

I was relaxing in the company of my sisters on Christmas afternoon when my husband appeared with an expression of deep concern on his face. "I don't know how to tell you", he said, "but the house has just collapsed!" In my enthusiasm to make the cake I hadn't realised the outer biscuit shapes, with the added weight of icing on the roof, needed an inner support of solid cake.

The family, and Belle, were happy to eat the ruins and the children for whom it was intended had to be satisfied with a photograph and a bag of leftover liquorice allsorts.

Belle

Culinary celebrations of Royal occasions

Many of you may recall that I mark most royal events by creating a special dish in celebration of the occasion. When the engagement of Prince Charles to Lady Diana Spencer was announced I created the Prince of Wales feathers using slices of boned chicken. I also created an elaborate gateau made from thin plates of sponge sandwiched together with cream and many of the fresh fruits in season. I called this Lady Diana Gateau. For the Royal wedding itself later that year I made a large wedding cake with photographs of the Prince and Lady Diana worked into the decoration. This cake was cut at our village street party on the evening of the wedding and the proceeds of a 'guess the weight' raffle I had arranged went towards a special summer outing for the Bisley Tuesday Club.

More recently I created a Royal crown in celebration of the birth of Prince William. I made this by elaborately icing and decorating a rich fruit cake with templates made from icing and covered with glitter of many colours to resemble the sparkle of diamonds and other precious stones. For the top of the cake I made a cradle and put a baby, trimmed with blue, inside. Nylon fur placed around the base of the cake was the best substitute I could find in the Stroud shops for ermin and the complete creation was placed on a blue velvet cushion. It looked very splendid until Belle, our golden retriever, who has a special passion for iced fruit cakes ate half of it after I had thoughtlessly left it at her eye level. As she lay under the kitchen table in absolute disgrace I realised I could not punish her further. You see, the Princess had produced just one baby son whereas Belle had recently produced six sons and a daughter and they were all noisily awaiting her motherly attention.

Belle's puppies

I continued to broadcast fortnightly with Severn Sound but I now had a newly employed female presenter who lost no time in cutting my half hour spot down to ten minutes, including the adverts. I found it difficult to adjust to this and decided the only way I could clearly get my recipes and shopping basket over in so short a time was to make a script. My experience at the BBC helped me set this up, although I was reluctant to do this. For one thing I felt it would take away the spontaneity of my broadcasts on which I had built up a reputation. Also reading over the air was a terrifying thought for me. The only way I overcame this was to spend much time reading my script over and over again so that by the time I got to the studio I knew it by heart and was able to speak it in a relaxed and natural manner, but it took up even more of my valuable time and demands on my time was now becoming a problem.

The only way to resolve this was to re-examine my situation and see where I could make a saving. In doing this it soon became clear that my demonstrations would have to be sacrificed. It was in the autumn of 1985 that I made this decision with great reluctance and not a little sorrow. I had been demonstrating my recipes at Bear House for seven years and many of those who regularly attended had become my friends. However, taking into account the number of hours I spent planning and preparing each demonstration I had to accept the point Adam had made from the beginning which was that financially they were not a viable proposition. They occupied too much of my time for the amount I could expect to receive in fees. Because of the limited space and facilities at Bear House I felt I could not expect people to pay more than the £5 fee I was now asking, but each demonstration demanded a similar amount of time and energy regardless as to the numbers attending and my kitchen only seated 12. I was never greedy for money, any financial gain was a bonus. I did not have to do my demonstrations, I chose to do them and in doing so freely gave up my time in order to pass on my talent. I hoped I might keep my hand in by demonstrating for fund-raising events and to sixth form colleges. Meanwhile my writing and broadcasting had to take priority and the extra time I now had could be spent promoting these newly found skills in an effort to reach a wider audience.

9

But even the best laid plans have a habit of going wrong and not long after I had made this decision we received news that Adam's aunt Nora (Ra) had been diagnosed with a terminal illness. She had had no children of her own and I decided to spend as much time as I could with her. The visits became longer and more frequent and at the end of one particularly tiring day I had a telephone call from Adam. "You have a letter here" he said, "It looks as though it's from the broadcasting company." I was immediately suspicious. I never had letters from them, everything had always been arranged verbally, whatever could this be? "I'll open it shall I" said Adam, and before I had time to say "no, please leave it until I come home" he continued...... "Oh dear, it's bad news for you I'm afraid, they don't want you any more" and he read "Dear Mo, in order to help you forward plan your own arrangements for the New Year, I am writing in good time to let you know that we have made a decision to rest your spot from after Christmas. Thank you for your hard work and professionalism over the past years........." I later discovered the local gas board had agreed a lot of advertising and part of the agreement was that one of their staff would fill the cookery spot. It was a commercial radio station and needed advertising fees to keep going – I could not compete against this. I had enjoyed it so much and would have done it for nothing had I been given the opportunity.

I was really saddened by this news and away from the warmth and comfort of my home and family I spent many hours before sleep would come thinking about the contents of the letter and about my future, if indeed I had a future as a cook. I had given up my demonstrations and every attempt I had made to get other work had been refused. I had written to the BBC in Bristol and this time I was offered an interview which I attended but the person who had offered me the interview was not expected in that day and there was nothing in her diary about an interview with me – I had been there before, I remembered!

Following an article in a national newspaper I wrote to Michael Smith, at that time and until his sudden death, a well-known writer and T.V. cookery personality. His reply was encouraging, it read – "You're certainly on the right tack in the way you present yourself – excellent. What you now need is a good agent and a P.R. person to handle promotional work. May I suggest........." He gave a name but no address or telephone number and all attempts I made to obtain this by telephone and letter remained unanswered until I eventually gave up.

I had written to every possible outlet, magazines, newspapers, I could find in an attempt to get work but my efforts resulted in rejections from a handful and total silence from the majority. I had to face facts. I was only one in hundreds, possibly thousands of people all over the country trying to sell their cooking skills. What made me think I had anything better to offer than anyone else? Clearly I had not.

I had spent most of my life cooking and creating recipes. I had worked really hard over the past years presenting my demonstrations and carrying out all work I was offered with complimentary and pleasing results. I could not believe that so suddenly and from a letter read out at the end of a telephone line, it had all come to an end. But it hadn't all come to an end, I still had my column and in the early hours of that morning it all became clear to me – writing and cooking are two skills which in many ways are similar, when you write you juggle with words and when you cook you juggle with ingredients. Why don't I combine my writing and cooking skills and write a cookery book? The many who had attended my cookery demonstrations had so often said how they wished they could have my recipes in a book. I have little to lose and if it were successful it might finally rid me of that childhood bee that settled in my bonnet.

But it didn't work out quite like that. The headaches Adam had been experiencing were becoming more frequent and he arrived home from the office one evening to say that he had received a telephone call from his eye specialist. The head scan he had recently had revealed a large tumour. From that moment my life changed. An appointment had been made with a brain surgeon at Frenchay Hospital in Bristol, and within days he underwent surgery.

This was the result of two years of wrong diagnosis. Although on our first interview with the surgeon we were assured the tumour would not be malignant, because of its size it was a much more major operation than had been thought. The family has always come first and everything connected with my cooking was immediately put on hold. When Adam eventually came home from hospital he was very weak and frail, a very sick man and in need of much care. The situation was further aggravated when he was visited, within days of returning home, by his managing director with the devastating news that he had lost his job – I felt so sorry for that man, this task was not of his making and it was clearly distressing to him. It was now evident that over the past months Adam had not been able to do his job properly, a tough new management team had recently taken over the company and in the words of Alan Sugar, decided "you're fired."

I wondered if Adam would ever be well enough to work again – the future was too hard to contemplate, so I tried not to do so. Ed now just 20 was suddenly the only wage earner in the family. Having realised he wasn't going to jump from his A level desk into a Formula 1 racing car, he was doing an apprenticeship with the owner of the local garage. Bill and Nell were still at private school, and were each awaiting A and O level results. The day before Adam was admitted to hospital for the operation I had driven Helen to Heathrow to begin a French exchange, she would be returning two weeks later with the French student, Armide de Luppe who would spend the next two weeks with us. This, as it now happened, coincided with Adam's return home from hospital. Friends helped with entertaining Armide. I was relieved when the day arrived for her return home, although this turned out to be a day full of unexpected events, and a day which still exhausts me to remember.

I woke early and remembered the joint of bacon I had put into the oven to simmer for an hour – at least twelve hours earlier! This now very reduced joint was needed for supper that evening. It was the morning of Nell's expected O level results, the post arrived but with no envelope for Nell – she was 'upset', to put it very mildly! As the morning progressed the telephone line became hot with calls from friends relating their results and enquiring about Nell's. In an attempt to calm the situation I rang Nell's school, the Convent, and asked if they could give me Helen's results. No they could not, under no circumstances did they give results over the telephone, I could come to school where all results would be on the notice board, otherwise they felt sure they would arrive in the next post, or the next day – try telling this to a 16 year old awaiting O level results! I tried to explain to them the pressure I was under and how I could not possibly come to school that day which was a good hour's drive away. Very reluctantly they reviewed the situation and said all they could say was that they felt sure Helen would be pleased with her results – it did little to calm my irate teenage daughter.

During Armide's stay with us she had especially enjoyed a pudding I had served and which she had watched me make. In return she wished very much to show me how to make a French tarte tatin. This was her last morning with us, I had all the ingredients and it seemed unkind not to let her make the tart. Amongst all the chaos, many in and outgoing telephone calls, lunch to prepare and leave for Adam, sandwiches to make for us, I tried to concentrate on the making of the pudding. Adding to all this was Bill's concern to get on the road. He had an interview with Kingston Polytechnic in the hope of a place with them to read Geography. The interview was at 3.30 pm. that very afternoon. We eventually set out for the airport and the interview, Bill, having just passed his driving test, at the wheel. We arrived at Heathrow in good time for the 3 pm. flight and leaving Bill in the car, Nell and I escorted Armide to the departure lounge. We were directed to a room especially reserved for youngsters travelling with an assistant to see them safely on the plane. This room seemed to be in the bowels of the terminal building. We checked in and were told to sit and wait. We were joined from time to time by other travelling youngsters. The clock ticked by, 2.30 pm.–2.40 pm.–2.45 pm. At 2.50 pm. I became a little anxious, not only about Armide missing her flight and having to return home with us, but about Bill's important interview in Kingston at 3.30 pm. I rang the bell on the desk, the approaching stewardess could not believe what she saw – "why are you all still here, you should be on the plane?" She gathered up the youngsters, rushed them through the door and, presumably to the waiting flight. That was the last we saw of Armide. Nell and I found our way to the car but there was no Bill. Frantic with worry about his interview and afraid he would miss the opportunity of a place by not turning up on time, he had gone in search of us. We all eventually got into the car at around 3 pm. the only words of comfort I could think of to say were, "Don't worry Bill, we're not late yet!"

Directing Bill through the centre of Kingston in the Friday evening rush hour traffic was an interesting experience and we eventually arrived at the appointed building. Some time later William returned to the car with a broad smile. He had been offered a place. As we pulled on to the M4 the heavens opened and for a few minutes hail stones the size of marbles almost brought the traffic to a standstill, Bill was in the fast lane, of course.

We arrived home to a kitchen full of lads, all waiting to see Bill, to hear his news and to celebrate their results. Adam staggered into the kitchen looking tired and confused, and Ed returned from the garage, grinning from ear to ear, wearing his oily overalls as always, and speaking his now familiar words describing his hunger pains, "Mother, I'm

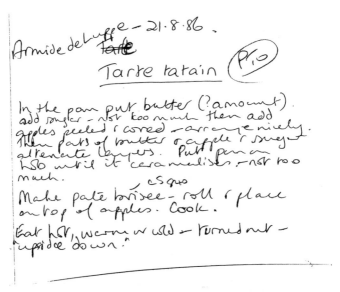

Recipe as dictated by Armide and cooked before leaving for Heathrow

ravishing" – yes, everybody was hungry, it was time to get supper. Before getting into bed I thanked God for bringing us all safely to the end of another day and was asleep almost before my head touched the pillow.

Our financial situation was bleak and during the coming weeks and months I would often wake fearing we would have to leave our beloved Bear House. I tried to think how I could earn some money. I still had my shorthand and typing skills, but secretarial positions were so different from when I first qualified and in any case who would look after Adam? Who would keep all the domestic chores going? No, taking a job was out of the question. One day I noticed in the window of a new shop in Stroud some shiny red boxes roughly the size of a four inch cube. I examined these and decided I could make small Christmas cakes to fit inside and sell them. The owner of the shop kindly gave me the telephone number of the couple importing these from America, also paper bags of attractive colours and a range of sticky backed labels. I made decorated Christmas cakes to fit the boxes and tied them with gold ribbon. I made fudge of a variety of flavours and filled them into bags of different colours. I then drove round Gloucestershire selling my wares. It was all so unfamiliar to me and I cannot say I enjoyed it but I did secure a number of orders and spent the weeks leading up to Christmas making, packaging and delivering my confections. Although they looked very attractive when ready for delivery, it was time consuming and tiring work and after Christmas orders went into decline.

Eventually Adam became stronger and was able to join a

computer course. But this concerned me. He had only a few months earlier undergone a most serious operation followed by six weeks of daily radiotherapy, and was now having to get up in time to leave the house at 7 am. in order to get to the course in the centre of Gloucester for 8 am. until 4 pm. Unable to drive for a while, I took and collected him daily. After the course he purchased an Amstrad computer with the idea of setting up his own accountancy practice from home. But it was Ra to whom we were most grateful. On her death she left her estate to Adam. This relieved us of the immediate impending financial disaster and enabled us to continue living at Bear House.

Adam's operation took its toll in many ways and resulted in a totally different life style for me. I soon realised I was going to have to take on much more household responsibility, payment of bills and accounts, all the things I had never shown an interest in, I now had to understand and do. Every aspect of running a household, domestic and social, was up to me. And then there was the garden, which had been much neglected. I needed all the energy and stamina I could muster and it was the garden which gave me solace and kept me going. I spent every available minute out there uprooting and repositioning plants, buying and planting new shrubs because they took my fancy regardless as to whether they would grow in the shade or light, or where I had chosen to put them. Filling in beds and making paved areas to cut down on the work for the future. I redesigned the whole garden into little areas rather like rooms in a house where we could follow sun or shade and look always, on our beloved Bear House, our peaceful haven. In cool or wet weather I escaped into the greenhouse sowing seeds and pricking them out to grow on before planting them into pots and borders. Climbing steps and ladders and pruning back great shrubs and hedges which had been neglected for years, my energy seemed inexhaustible. Our dear neighbour and friend Basil Weaving, a wonderful gardener, encouraged and taught me a lot and together we developed two small areas where I was able to grow early potatoes, courgettes and runner beans. Cut and come again lettuces, spinach, dwarf beans, land cress and rocket and any other salad ingredient I could find a space for. As I was sowing and planting I was always thinking of how I might use these in my cooking and develop new recipes. Gardening became a passion which almost took over from my love of cooking.

After a busy day in the garden my energy sapped on entering the kitchen but there was still a meal to get. And so my Lazy Cook recipes developed. No longer did I have time, or energy, to do the sort of cooking which I had grown up with and which for many years had demonstrated. I recognised it was more important than ever that we should eat good, healthy meals, but clearly something had to be sacrificed. I began by taking a new look at the present day ingredients available to me both in my store cupboard and on the supermarket shelves. Putting all my experience to the test, taking short cuts and speeding up on preparation and assembly, I developed a completely new way of preparing and presenting my meals, still tasty, nutritious, and good to look at but very quick to prepare.

My kitchen window is on a narrow section of road with passing people and traffic. Friends and neighbours would ask me, "What are you doing these days, you are always in your kitchen, you are always cooking?" To which I would answer, "No, I spend very little time in the kitchen nowadays, I have many other things to do and spend a lot of time in the garden, when I get into the kitchen I am very lazy." And so this word lazy caught on and I began to call myself the Lazy Cook and wrote my thoughts about it.

After a while Adam was able to do a little work and started his own practice from home. I began to think again about the book I had decided to write and set about doing it. At every available opportunity I would set up the portable typewriter on the kitchen table and tap away. It told the story of my life as a cook, much as I have done here, and included many recipes. I sent it to the Dorling Kindersley agent I had met at the Lionel Blue interview. After several weeks he returned my manuscript together with a letter from Dorling Kindersley part of which read – "The book will be charming, but I am sure it is wrong for DK, it would not have world market appeal …" After this and rejections from a handful of other publishing houses, it was put to rest on the shelf.

I had continued to write my monthly column for the magazine until a sudden takeover resulted in my recipe column being dropped and I was invited to cover the wine and dine page. This meant dining at a restaurant and writing my comments on it. It was an exciting new venture not least for me, but for Adam and friends hopeful of an opportunity to join me in a free meal! It further tested my writing skills and I enjoyed the challenge, especially the memorable meal at Le Champignon Sauvage, the then newly opened French restaurant in Cheltenham. My review so pleased the chef, David Everitt-Matthias that he invited me to spend a day in his kitchen. The restaurant now has two Michelin stars and my review remains first in their album of reviews followed by those of well known restaurant critics. As for the magazine, sadly, after several takeovers, it folded as, of course, did my contribution as restaurant critic.

I continued to enjoy cooking for family and friends using my new Lazy recipes. Christmas, as always, was a big family occasion when we were joined by my two sisters and their families. There were many special treats to make, keeping up the traditions over the years. In addition there were, as always, cakes to make of varying sizes to take around the village to neighbours and friends. Beryl Warner, the wife of our late milkman, Clive, always said, "Christmas starts when Clive arrives home with Mo's Christmas cake." There were pounds of chocolates and fudge to give out or to package and send through the post, keeping back a selection for our own family party.

I tried my hand at outside catering and for three summers I cooked meals, including breakfast, coffee, lunch, tea and dinner for a group of 10 artists attending weekend and weekly teaching seminars run by friend and local artist Michael Edwards. After the first year I invited Annie Stevens to assist me. As always her help was invaluable and she often remarked, "I will never know how you coped with it all on your own." It was an interesting experience and many of the students requested my recipes. It made me think were I younger and in different circumstances, I might consider setting up a business in catering. It also made me think back to my first meeting with Sally Cox shortly after our arrival in Bisley, and the catering venture we attempted to set up, perhaps we should have put more effort into it.

On 16th October 1998 Adam had a further health set back when he suffered a small stroke and was forced to give up his practice. Feeling the need for even more economising I dusted down my sewing machine, an 18th birthday present from my parents, and brought it back into use. My maternal grandmother had been a seamstress in her youth and fortunately for me, I inherited some of her skills and always enjoyed sewing. Until I was old enough to use Grandma's old hand Singer sewing machine, I remember hand sewing outfits for my dolls, and as a teenager I had a go at designing anything from padded toilet bags to evening dresses. My employment with the BBC hadn't begun until a few days after my arrival in London and so, following Yvonne's advice, on my first morning in our Capital city I had enrolled for an evening class at the London College of Dress Design in Regent Street where I had studied design and pattern cutting. It was now many years since I had sewn but the time seemed opportune to take it up again. A morning would begin by cutting into a length of cloth bought from the excellent Yard's Ahead material shop in Stroud and, provided I had no interruptions, at the end of the day I would have a garment ready to wear, a copy of the latest designer wear but made for a fraction of the price.

And so time went by . . .

Mary (née Mattock) and myself

Stella (L), Stanley and myself

Yvonne – October 2006

Denise (née Cox)

Annie (née Graham)

Ed and Esme

Nell and Robin's wedding
cake stored in refrigerator

Making bouquets for Nell
and Robin's wedding

Nell and Robin

Bill and Lynn

Nell dressed for their
Hindu wedding

Adam and myself – our 40th
wedding anniversary lunch

Audrey and Freddie before our
proposed visit to Thurlestone

Celebrating Adam's 75th birthday

Bear House garden

The Lazy Cook with young
admirers

Making caramel baskets in the
kitchen of Le Champignon Sauvage

Book signing at WH Smith,
Stroud

A Lazy Cook's Summer on sale at
Waitrose

My new office

My office in
the hall

A corner of Bear House
kitchen

Belle our golden retriever

Royal wedding cake

'Crown' cake to celebrate the
birth of Prince William

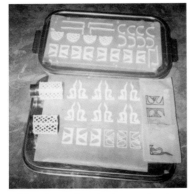

Templates for the 'crown' cake
and cradle

Gingerbread house

The first wedding cake I made

Cake to celebrate the 40th
anniversary meeting of the 'crowd'

Cake for a village wedding

Nell and Robin's cake in
the making

Coffee and walnut gateau

Christmas cakes and bags of
fudge and chocolates

Sparkling Dome

The Christmas turkey

Tray of home made chocolates

Praline meringue as made for my
first demonstration

Crystallized orange peel

Hand made roses and petals

Lazy Cook Quick Cauliflower Cheese in the au gratin dish bought 50 years ago

Dipping peppermint creams in chocolate

Chocolate Battenburg Cake

Part Two

FROM COOKER
TO COMPUTER

1

One day at the beginning of 1999 my friend Marie
Jennings invited me to coffee. Marie and her late husband
Professor Brian Locke had encouraged me over the years
and were always so interested to hear what I was doing, my
plans and hopes for the future, and gave me much valued
advice. Marie, who had had many books published, began
by saying "I know you have always hoped to have your
recipes published, why don't you do it yourself? With
modern computers it is possible to do this. You could have
100 copies printed, everyone in the village would buy one,
make it your millennium project." I came away thinking,
oh dear, what have I let myself in for now? How can I possibly write another book and furthermore publish it
myself? On the other hand Marie would think it pretty
wet of me if I ignored her advice, I must do something
about it. Why not? I have nothing to lose and it would
occupy these coming winter months when the garden is
dormant. It could be a way of promoting my new Lazy
Cook recipes. Without realising it at the time I was, from
that moment, venturing into a new career. Little did I
think that over the next four years I would write and

publish four books and sell thousands of copies alongside celebrity writers in bookshops and supermarkets country-wide. And little did I realise what a competitive market I was entering!

I did some research and then spent many hours at the kitchen table tapping away on the portable typewriter. I decided to call the book 'Enter the New Millennium with Lazy Cook Mo Smith – recipes, tips and anecdotes for the time pressured cook.' The opening chapter was headed 'Bisley over the past 1000 years – a potted history' and it talked of the changes in lifestyle and cooking in Bisley over the past century, and the recipes, mostly my latest Lazy Cook creations, were divided into sections to cover the period of Christmas, they included –

> 'Come for a weekend'
> 'A Lazy Cook's Christmas Day'
> 'Boxing Day – a meal after a walk'
> 'Let's have a party!'
> 'New Year's Eve dinner party'.

To keep the method short and simple I added at the end of each recipe some Lazy Cook tips – those important tips which I had learnt through experience and which would give confidence and ensure the success of the recipe – things like, "Don't worry if the sauce becomes lumpy, take the pan from the heat and whisk out the lumps, then continue cooking." Having completed the manuscript I read it through several times to check for mistakes. I honestly don't remember getting it proof-read by anyone else, such a thing never occurred to me – ignorance is bliss! Then I had to find a printer and by chance I discovered James Douglas owner of the Leckhampton Printing Company in Cheltenham. James was able to recommend a type-setter and we discussed the quality of paper to be used. I chose bright red card for the cover which, below the title, showed a drawing of Bear House and the pages were held together with staples.

Then followed endless visits to and from the printer checking and adding more corrections until it eventually went to press. I didn't order Marie's suggested 100 copies, but 1,000!

The printed book was ready by the beginning of November. I was so excited and quite unphased that I had just a few weeks to sell one thousand books! I offered them to local shops and village post offices, I wrote letters and sent copies to all the local newspaper editors, and to friends, family and all who had attended my cookery demonstrations over the years and who had repeatedly asked, "Why can't we have your recipes in a book?"

I had priced the book at £2.50 per copy and offered to donate 50p from each sale to charity. In the letter I stated that if 10 copies were purchased (postage and package included), I would send a cheque for £5.00 made out to a charity of their choice. Orders and cheques came flooding in and by the end of the year I had sold all but a handful of my books – I was overjoyed.

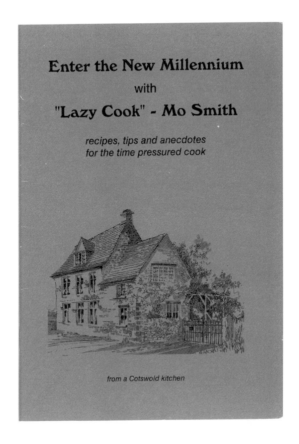

Enter the New Millennium

with

"Lazy Cook" ~ Mo Smith

recipes, tips and anecdotes
for the time pressured cook

from a Cotswold kitchen

At the beginning of the year 2000 I thought about my little red cookery book and the ease with which I had sold 1,000 copies, mostly within the area of Gloucestershire. No one else knew of my Lazy Cook recipes. I had many more recipes and was creating them all the time, why didn't I do another book? For this second book I had new ideas, the most ambitious of which was to sell it through the major bookshops and supermarkets and for this reason it would have to be perfect bound and include a bar code and ISBN (International Standard Book Number).

I decided on the title 'Lazy Cook in the Kitchen' and daughter Nell suggested the additional words, 'mouth-watering recipes for the time-pressured cook' and sketched out a girl in a hammock as an appropriate logo. I was recommended to a local artist who did the book cover design and with Nell's approval selected a design and colour. I felt I could no longer expect the local building society to accept the volume of cheques I had been paying into my account, so I went to see the bank manager and opened a Lazy Cook account.

Typing recipes was the least favourite part of compiling the book, it was so time-consuming and demanded absolute concentration. The portable typewriter lacked the facility to quickly erase mistakes, to add or change words and sentences, and it became a very long and boring process. I gazed at Adam's Amstrad computer and wondered if I dared ask if I could use it!

Never let a husband teach you to drive, never let a husband teach you to use a computer!

Was it really going to be any quicker than my dependable little portable typewriter? Well yes, of course it was, eventually! The trouble was that my manuscript was using up a lot of space and 'saving' on the Amstrad could take an eternity. One day disaster struck, it crashed under the strain and I lost all my work. This really was bad news, it was now well into April and because I had sub-headed the title 'Autumn to Easter' I needed to have the book printed by the beginning of September at the latest. How naive I was. I was soon to learn that book buyers choose their stock months in advance of a coming season. Our eldest son Ed was updating his computer and was pleased to let me have the redundant model, with Microsoft Word 98 – it sounded so grand and I felt I really had entered the modern computer age. But it was as different as chalk and cheese from the Amstrad and it meant learning all over again. I would rise early to make a good start only to be frustrated by it taking me anything up to half an hour simply to find a new page! With much help from many friends and endless patience from local computer man Roger Fouske I got my head around it.

What an asset it was to be able to 'touch type', my fingers tapped away at an unbelievable pace, and eventually the manuscript was complete and ready to take to printer James. Perfect binding was no problem, a bar code was no problem, the typesetter can do those said James. An ISBN was a problem. I rang Marie for advice and she said, not to worry; Brian can let you have one of those. Although greatly relieved and extremely grateful, I was also surprised that they could provide me with this, what amazing people they were, what contacts they must have!

This time friends Bobbie Revell and Annie Stevens helped me to proof read until, after many evenings of concentrated reading, followed by many trips to and from the type setter, all was ready, except for the barcode. On my final visit to the type-setter I said "It must have a bar code, James tells me you can supply one." "Yes, I can do them", he said, "no problem, just give me the numbers." The numbers? "I don't have any numbers, don't you provide those?" No, he didn't and had no idea where they came from. What a disaster, I couldn't believe it. It was now the beginning of August, the book I had hoped to have in the shops by now was not even ready for print. I telephoned Marie who gave me the London name and number of a company who supplied barcodes. On ringing them they said it would cost £140. My husband thought this was a ridiculous amount of money and I should refuse to pay it, but I had little choice, until I thought of 'yellow pages'. Searching under 'barcodes' I found a company in Banbury, Oxfordshire. My telephone call was answered by a friendly voice, "Yes, we supply barcodes, how many do you need?" I asked, how much they were. £11 each came the reply. I couldn't believe it. "Do they work" I asked. "Yes, of course they work!" came the surprised answer, she had clearly never been asked such a question before, "we supply thousands of them. Would you like it on film or would you like me to email it to your printer?" These questions were like a foreign language to me but at the end of the day all was sorted and I was only too pleased to send a cheque for £11. The final decisions were how much to price the book and how many to print. I decided on £5.50 per copy with a percentage given from each sale to charity. James and I debated on how many to print and on the strength of the previous sales we decided on 5,000 copies.

Feeling in need of a break, Adam and I booked a week in a small hotel near Tenby in Wales. Walking along the beach one day we met the Letts family, Quentin and Lois and their children who at that time lived near Bisley. Lois asked me how my writing was going and I said my new book was being printed as we spoke. "Great", she said, "how many are you having printed?" When I said 5,000 copies her face changed. "5,000, most publishers would print a first run of 2,000 at most!" Undaunted by this remark, which was kindly meant, I continued to enjoy the holiday. Some time after we had returned home, Adam said, "Where are you going to store these books? Have you any idea what 5,000 books looks like? You can't store them in the house, they will be too heavy!" On my next visit to James I mentioned this, to which he replied, "Not to worry, I can store them here" – what a relief.

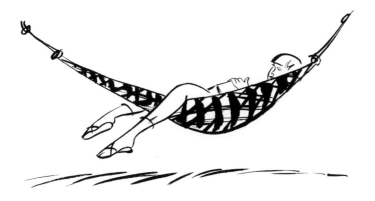

2

The most important thing to remember before venturing into self publishing, a tip I now pass on to authors who are thinking about this is, you must have absolute confidence in your subject before you begin because, as copies roll from the printing press there is only one person to sell them and that is you. I was entering one of the most competitive markets there was. It is even more so now and is dominated by an ever growing number of celebrity writers and television chefs – how was I going to enter that market and sell my books? I had no publisher, no agent, and my books had no pictures. Those were the negative thoughts. On the positive side I was sure of my product and convinced there was a market out there for my kind of cooking. I knew my 'Lazy Cook' title was good and I had followed advice and registered it. I also felt the layout of my book, including little story lines, and the Lazy Cook tips that were given at the end of each recipe, was different from anything on the market at that time. My recipes were created from my many years of experience as a cook, and now as a cook pressured for time they took on a new twist, recommending off the shelf and ready prepared ingredients such as no other book or television cook featured at that time. I recommended the use of ready-baked pastry and pastry cases to which your own choice of savoury or sweet fillings can be added with no fear of the chosen ingredient seeping out from a crack in a home made case and ending up on the floor of the oven. I rarely recommended sauces made from a roux base but made in minutes perhaps using a jar of piccalilli whizzed up in a food processor to make a mustard sauce; garlic or peppered Boursin cheese melted with a little milk, or one of the many pastes now available, sundried tomato, tapenade, olive and so on, melted down with the addition of wine, cream, stock or cooking juices. I recommended oven chips to add an instant topping to a Cottage or Shepherds Pie – so much quicker than peeling, cooking, mashing or slicing potatoes, and no washing up! Ready grated chocolate to scatter directly on to cakes hot from the oven – so much quicker than grating or melting chocolate and spreading it over the cake. For quick desserts I used large jars of blackcurrants to make instant crumbles or my increasingly popular Blackcurrant Trifle which can be made in minutes. Taking these short cuts and speeding up on preparation and assembly was central to my Lazy cooking. Recommending how to get the best out of ingredients and illustrating how a handful of ingredients can be prepared and presented in so many different ways resulting in a variety of colours, textures and flavours. Yes, my recipes I was sure, were different in the year 2000 and I was confident my new book would sell.

I began my quest by 'cold calling' on local shops, whether part of a multiple chain or a small privately owned bookshop. I never telephoned first, that would have given the buyer the opportunity to say "No thank you" before even seeing the goods. With luck I was able to see the buyer and from that first moment of meeting I could read their interest, or otherwise. Their approach, their tone of voice, the way they handled the book, if at all. These were the pointers which I felt reflected their professionalism and their interest in my work.

One of my first orders came from the then manager of the Stroud branch of W.H.Smith. Listening to me, then after flicking through the pages of my book, the cover, front and back, he invited me into his office. He began. "Should I decide to buy your book have you any idea of the terms and conditions of sale my company will impose?" No, I had no idea. He then asked. "How many books have you had printed?" When I told him 5,000 copies he looked aghast and after a slight hesitation said. "Would you like to do a signing? I could set it up for you in a few weeks time to catch the Christmas trade." I felt I had been rocketed to celebrity status!

John Evans, buyer at the recently opened branch of Ottakars in Cirencester greeted me like a long lost friend. "Come this way" he said, and escorted me to the cookery book section. "I will put a special display of your books here, front facing, so that they can be easily seen." Over the years he has continued his enthusiasm and compliments about my books and my recipes. Some years later in a Christmas card depicting the three wise men he wrote – "Here are three wise men bearing gifts – all rather extravagant and not at all down-to-earth and practical like your books. Well done."

Other buyers were not so welcoming and enthusiastic. I remember one cold wet day parking my car and finding my way through the streets of a small local town in search of a newly opened bookshop to which I had been recommended. The proprietor examined my book. "Um ... nice cover, good title, good price." My optimism of a good sale was increasing, until I heard, "I'll take one!" And so I walked back to the car to get a new copy and my book of invoices. Would she, I wondered, pay today, or expect it on sale or return? But then life is tough for small book shop owners, even at that time, and more so now.

Having got my book into many shops in the Gloucestershire area, the next step was to get publicity through newspapers and magazines so that the public might read about me and go in search of my book. Similarly, by getting my book into the shops, especially a local branch of a national chain, would give it kudos with the result that a newspaper or magazine editor might be more likely to give it space – it was a chicken and egg situation about which I was rapidly learning.

At about this time I was approached by BBC Radio Gloucestershire and began regular broadcasts of my recipes with them. The producers would come to my kitchen and record me creating whatever recipes I had chosen. Cooking and talking in front of an audience who can see what you are doing requires a certain skill, cooking and explaining what you are doing to a radio audience requires a very different skill. When air time is limited trying to make what you are doing sound exciting and to hold the listener's interest, even though sometimes I might not have all the necessary ingredients to hand, demanded great concentration and was very challenging. Even so I continued these recordings until quite recently. Broadcasting still gives me a buzz, an excitement, and whether it is live or recorded, the adrenalin flows.

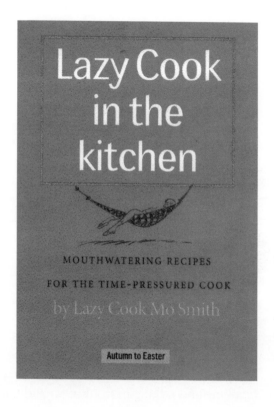

3

My next target was to promote my book nationally. I began by writing letters to editors of national newspapers and magazines enclosing a complimentary copy of my book to which, to my great disappointment I had no response. Daughter Nell who had decided on a career in marketing, advised me, "No point in sending a letter Mummy, nobody answers letters these days you must email people." Email? I had just about mastered the art of cutting and pasting, the thought of emailing sent me into complete panic! But it had to be done and guidance from more computer literate friends than myself, often directed from the telephone, helped me sort this. You must follow up your emails and letters with a telephone call, advised Nell. More easily said than done. After much searching for telephone numbers, then being passed around from office to office I might eventually hear the voice of the editor, but more often than not a message on an answer machine and I soon learnt there was little point in leaving a message, they were rarely answered. After many attempts, and when least expected, or prepared, the person I was seeking would answer my call, but often to no avail. As with the shop book buyers, the tone of the voice at the end of the line became a clear indication as to whether they would choose to feature the book. Some were really helpful and even though they could not feature my book at that moment they let me down lightly and in a non patronising manner. Most immediately answered, "We only feature the celebrity titles." What was a girl to do? The answer – pick oneself up and press on! I would often take a walk, potter in the garden or sit and talk to Adam who would make me laugh and feel wanted and I would eventually return to the computer refreshed and brimming with renewed enthusiasm.

As well as the book chains, most supermarkets were now selling cookery books. I spoke with the manager of the recently opened branch of Waitrose in Stroud where I had become a regular shopper. He suggested that I contact their Head Office from where all the buying was done. After many telephone calls and, as with the media, being passed from one person to another, ("going round the houses" I now call it!) I managed to speak with the cookery book buyer who suggested I send a copy of my book to her office. "At least she hasn't turned me down" were my immediate thoughts, "and she has asked to see my book, perhaps I'm in with a chance!" Like the cat chasing the mouse, I telephoned this buyer on a fairly regular basis, and was told she was still thinking about it – dare I continue to hope? My next telephone call was answered by a very jubilant sounding voice "Oh hello, no I haven't decided yet and I'm going on holiday tomorrow for two weeks, goodbye." What was I to make of this? She still had not said no, and her tone and words were more friendly than ever before. I noted the date of her return from holiday in my diary.

It was with great trepidation that I made the next telephone call. Until now I had been able to hang on to the hope that she would buy my book, she must surely make a decision soon, was today going to be one of great disappointment? My call was answered by the now familiar sounding voice but a different name, my buyer had got married, hence the reason for the jubilation when we last spoke. Hello Mo, "Yes", she said, "I've decided to buy your book, it will be in all our stores countrywide. You will be hearing from Gardners our distributors with whom you will be asked to sign a contract." All I could think to say was, thank you, thank you, thank you! I ran into the garden and met Adam in the drive. I was grinning from ear to ear, dancing up and down and both thumbs in the air, but such was the effect it had on me that I could not speak, I could not tell him my news but he knew it was something good by my actions. My first telephone call was to Nell who was equally elated. "Mummy that's wonderful news, well done, how many do they want? When do they want them? What discount do they want?" To which I had no answers, I hadn't asked any of these important questions. I still had much to learn.

The prospect of my book being sold in all branches of a supermarket gave power to my elbow and I decided to approach national newspapers and magazines again in the hope of Christmas sales. I had overlooked the fact that we were now well into October 2000, their projected arrangements for Christmas were going to press and they were now concentrating on next year's Easter and summer features. As my book was sub-headed 'Autumn to Easter' I had missed further promotion until the autumn of 2001 by which time I was planning to be writing my next book, 'A Lazy Cook's Summer'!

I had expected 'Lazy Cook in the Kitchen' to appear in Waitrose before Christmas, but it was well into December before I had a telephone call from Gardners, the book distributors I had been told would contact me. During this telephone conversation their terms of sale were made clear – all orders were placed on a 'sale or return' basis, the commission they requested had to be agreed, I had to cover the cost of carriage, payment would be made 90 days following the date of invoice – as my daughter reminded me, "You are with the big boys now Mummy." But I needed them, they were the gateway to getting my books into the major stores and supermarkets. As an unknown self-publisher I was privileged to have an account with them and over the years I have built up a good relationship with many members of their staff who have been so helpful and encouraging to me. Having until now sold books in quantities of five or ten copies, I felt a great sense of achievement when, one day, I opened an email containing an order for 500 books. Even so it was not until the week before Easter that my 'Lazy Cook in the Kitchen' first appeared in the Waitrose store in Stroud.

It was a tremendous thrill to see my book on sale in a major store and alongside those of celebrities and television chefs ... but would the public buy? I constantly reminded myself that the books were on sale or return and each time I went into the store I would take a sideways glance at the cookery book shelves. To my dismay there always seemed to be the same number of my books on display. I was devastated and concluded no one was buying because of the 'Autumn to Easter' sub-title – why had I chosen to add this? I decided I should introduce myself to the buyer, perhaps I could do something to encourage sales. The buyer greeted me with great enthusiasm, "It's so good to meet you and your books are selling like hot cakes." she said, "I've just placed yet another order with Gardners." What a relief, I could hold my head high and enjoy the euphoria.

But there was no time to waste, emails must be sent to the media, nationally and locally, announcing my self-published book was now on sale at all branches of a major supermarket, surely this was worthy of a feature? Not necessarily so! Many hours spent making telephone calls still produced the now familiar message "I'm sorry, we only feature celebrities." It was all part of the learning process, and it all adds to the work load. But I remembered it was a chicken and egg situation; the public would read about me, see my book and would buy it, and vice versa. I needed both buyers and the media on my side.

May 2001 gave me something other than my book sales to think about. It was a month of great joy for us all with the first family wedding. We all travelled to Scotland where Bill and Lynn were married in St. Patrick's Church, Dumbarton (Lynn's home town), followed by a reception at The Roman Camp Hotel, Callender. What a happy and memorable occasion it was after which, accompanied by

Audrey and Freddie we travelled up country and spent a week in the Highlands.

Suddenly it was summer and the shops, and my salad garden, were alive with new seasonal ingredients and with these my creative instincts came to the fore. Over the months many new summer recipes were to be created for that new book I had in mind – 'A Lazy Cook's Summer'.

4

Having tasted success with one supermarket I now decided to target another. I had written emails and made many telephone calls to the head office of Sainsbury's and one day I managed to speak to the cookery book buyer. I realised from the tone of her voice that I might be in with a chance. She requested a copy of my book, which was further encouragement. She always received my telephone calls in a friendly manner and one day asked where I lived. When I said "a village called Bisley, Nr. Stroud," she said, "oh I know Bisley, my sister lived for a short while in a nearby village, I remember visiting Bisley quite often". Another time she said, "Do you think you could come to our Head Office in London one day? I would like to meet you."

A few weeks later I took a train and made my way to the new Sainsbury's Head Office in Holborn. I was pleased to be early for the appointment so I stopped for a coffee and gave myself time to think about the meeting. I had my writing pad and a list of questions I might ask, as suggested by Nell. Still aware that first impressions are important

I was pleased that on calling at the village shop to pick up a newspaper before driving to the station, I met friend and neighbour Jane Bentley. "You're looking good," was her greeting, "going somewhere important?" This eased my fears and any doubts I had about wearing the right thing.

Once again I was at a crossroads, it was decision time, would I leave with a feeling of elation or rejection? Suddenly I felt completely inadequate and out of my depth. Not for the first time in my life I had got myself into this unbelievable situation. How did I expect my recipes to compete with the new books flooding the market, books written by celebrity chefs and other well-known personalities? Hard back books with stunning pictures illustrating how dishes should look. Most of these were published by newly formed and powerful publishing conglomerates with teams of marketing expertise and agents to promote and sell the books. What chance did I have? Who did I think I was? What was I doing here? I longed to be back at Bear House! Then I pulled myself together and began again to think more positively. I reminded myself of the first principles of selling – you must be sure of your product. My sales were good and improving. The very fact that one national supermarket was already selling my book and at the end of this interview I might have a second on board was further proof of this. Anyone can sell their book if they have a television series and a well-known publisher and agent behind them. I have done all this myself. Created the recipes, written, edited and published my book. The feedback I was receiving from grateful readers and time-pressured cooks of all ages convinced me that I had a good product, I just needed to get it out there to the public at large. My confidence returned, I had earned the right to be there, there was no other book like mine on the market, my recipes were unique and right for this new century.

My watch told me it was time to head for this new imposing building and meet the buyer in whose hands my fate lay. I reminded myself of our last telephone conversation when this interview was arranged. It had, as always, been of a friendly and encouraging tone and I felt sure it would be a good meeting, whatever the outcome.

At the reception desk I was given a security badge to wear and asked to sit in the waiting area on the right, and to help myself to refreshments. What a waiting area! It reminded me of the foyer of a luxury hotel. Low round tables with easy chairs filled most of the space. Many of these were already occupied by important looking people, and all very young, None appeared to have writing pads, but 'personal organisers' which the family has tried to persuade me to use ... perhaps I should have taken their advice? A few had the latest in modern computer technology – a laptop. Along one wall was a splendid assortment of refreshments and drinks of all kinds and worthy of a luxury hotel. Having just had coffee I was happy to find an empty table, grabbed a newspaper and tried to look relaxed whilst pretending to do the crossword, and wait.

After a short while a young couple arrived, suitably equipped as already described. There being no other free tables they asked if I minded if they joined me. They were soon greeted by an obvious member of Sainsbury's Staff who said, "It's a little early, our interview room isn't booked for another ten minutes, help yourselves to refreshments, I'll be back shortly." Did I hear correctly? Did he say an interview room? They must be really important. I looked up from my newspaper to see a young lady approaching me. "Is it Mo?" We shook hands and exchanged the usual pleasantries, how was my journey? Did I find the building easily? etc then she said, "Would you mind waiting while I see if I can book an interview room?" The effect of this was like being transported to a different planet and I felt really important, for a minute, until I remembered she hadn't actually booked a room. Was I not so important? What if they didn't have a room available? I looked around to see if there might be a corner in which we could have our interview. My doubts were unfounded, there was a room and soon we were walking down a long corridor with many numbered, closed doors on either side until we eventually found the one allocated to us. It was like a small board room and had all the necessary equipment needed for a meeting. It was ours for 30 minutes.

My book was put on the table and I was asked how I had written it, how I got the idea for it, how I created my recipes, what had inspired me to write and publish my own book? She then said, "I will be perfectly honest with you," (here comes the gentle let down I thought), but she continued, "I receive, on average, 40 cookery books a month. Most of them I don't even bother to open, they all look the same and I know the recipes will all be the same. On the morning your book arrived it immediately caught my attention. The colour, the title, everything was different from anything I had seen before. I opened it and looked at the layout and the recipes, I was immediately impressed. I could make these recipes, yes, I liked it, yes I am going to buy your book." I didn't know whether to kiss her or to cry, I was so elated. I remembered the list of questions I had and asked how many books might she order. "How long is a piece of string," came the reply. "I will place it in one module and see how it goes then move it around. You will receive the order from our book distributors, Cork International" (now no longer trading). Suddenly the door was opened, no it wasn't a cup of tea, but an official telling us our time was up – just like that! It was a bit, I imagined, like the end of a visit to a prison.

I walked on air as I made my way back to the underground station. Was this real? I couldn't wait to tell Adam and Nell and the boys. I looked at other pavement walkers and thought, "You might well be buying my cookery book soon!" I arrived at Paddington station much earlier than expected and realised I could catch an earlier train. I went to the enquiry desk to ask if I needed to pay extra and was told "yes, £19". This was very nearly as much as I had paid for the ticket for the return journey. No, I couldn't pay that and took myself off to have a coffee and people watch until my train was due. I reflected on the events of the day. My head was spinning with things to do, promotional emails to write to editors and book buyers, and many letters and telephone calls to make. I felt intoxicated with excitement and began to think about the quantity of books I might sell. My motivation had never come from how much money I might make, quite the contrary, as long as I had sufficient funds to pay the printing costs that was all that mattered. I had funded my first book, 'Enter the new Millennium' from my demonstration account and 'Lazy Cook in the Kitchen' had been paid for out of the profit made from sales of this first book. As I sipped my coffee I afforded myself the privilege of doing a rough calculation of how much profit I might make on the possible sales of one, two, or three thousand books and decided, yes, I could perhaps afford to upgrade my ticket and get the earlier train. By this time there was a long queue at the enquiry desk and the train was due to leave within a few minutes. I made my way to the barrier and asked to pay the extra to get this train. Neither railway official knew how to do this and called out to a nearby colleague for help. "Pay when you are on the train," was his advice, which I followed. I was tired and my thoughts were all over the place but I could not relax. Before the end of the journey the ticket collector came round. Handing over my ticket I said I believed I had to pay extra. After much tapping on his hand calculator, he replied "£3 please miss." I paid up and shut up.

Adam was sitting at the kitchen table with the late British Legion treasurer, Alan Birmingham. They had spent all day counting out the church collection following the annual Service of Remembrance the previous Sunday. My news to Adam had to go on hold. But I had to tell someone. I picked up telephone in the hall and rang Nell at her office. "Mummy you're a star, that is absolutely brilliant, well done, congratulations!"

All thoughts were now concentrated on Christmas sales. I

thought about my book, 'Enter the New Millennium'. That is a Christmas book, why don't I give it the new title 'A Lazy Cook's Christmas'? I made a note to ask Terry to design a new cover and James to perfect bind including barcode and ISBN. It would make an ideal stocking filler. Nell said, "Mummy don't do it, you have enough to do." But I didn't listen. It was the beginning of December before the books were printed. Local newspapers featured it and local shops took them but beyond that there was no chance of further promotion. Why had I not listened to my daughter? I also remembered Marie's comment, "It is a very good feeling to be able to say, sorry, I've sold all my books" Why, oh why, had I not listened? I then remembered Sainsbury's had opened a new store in Stroud. I went along and met a new, young duty manager. He thought my book was great, "Yes", he said, "I'll have some of these I'm sure they'll sell like hot cakes." Unfortunately for me, but even more so for him, they did not. The barcode had not gone through the Sainsbury's computer system and kept queues of impatient customers waiting at the check-out. Something had upset all the tills!!!!

Christmas came and went and no order was received from the Sainsbury's distributors. I was reluctant to keep bothering the buyer as she was a busy lady but it was several months since our meeting. My elation had simmered down and I began to wonder if she had forgotten her promise to buy my book. I was now writing my next book 'A Lazy Cook's Summer' and I would soon be writing to her about this in the hope she would buy it but with the promised order not yet received, was I being a little too optimistic? Suddenly, one day in February 2002, the telephone rang. It

was the Sainsbury's order, they would like 4,000 books –
celebration time again! My printer didn't have this many
books in stock and so I agreed to have a further 5,000
printed. With two supermarkets on board, it seemed we
might need these. I hadn't thought to ask the area covered
by the chosen module. The local branches of Sainsbury's
didn't have them but my sister Audrey was greatly surprised
when shopping in their Aberdeen store to see my book on
sale.

Despite many technical problems and a further change of computer, in May 2002 my next book 'A Lazy Cook's Summer' was ready to print. For this book I had my own ISBN. Although I was very grateful to Brian Locke for issuing me with ISBN's, it had always been a mystery to me that I had to quote "published by BriCor", when I was the publisher. I also felt it was an imposition on my part especially when Brian was sometimes telephoned by people enquiring about my books, or sending orders and cheques made out to BriCor.

I decided to make enquiries about obtaining ISBN's but from where? I looked through the Yellow Pages to find what seemed a big printing company based in Gloucester. I telephoned and having made my request the operator asked me to "Hold the line." Another voice asked, "Can I help you?" "Do you know from where I can obtain an ISBN", I asked. "No, but I know a man who does" came the instant reply. It was all so easy. I telephoned the given number and was asked, "How many would you like?" to which I replied, "One please." "The minimum is ten," came the reply followed by, "you can of course pass some on to other authors but, should you do so, they must quote "published by Mo Smith." The mystery was solved!

I discussed with James how many books to print. Waitrose had said they would buy this new book and hopefully Sainsbury's would also. My name was spreading, my Lazy Cook title was catching on, so we decided to print 10,000 copies!

I dropped a copy of this new book through the letterbox of Jane Bentley. Jane, a book editor by profession, has many times encouraged me and given me valued advice. A few days later she appeared at my kitchen door. "Mo, thank you. I love your new book. The choice of yellow for the cover is perfect for the summer and the recipes, although I've only quickly glanced at them, look yummy, and I thought, this would be good in YOU magazine, *The Mail on Sunday*. The editor, Sue Peart, is a friend of mine, I can't promise anything of course, but it so happens I'm meeting her for lunch tomorrow, would you like me to show it to her?" The YOU magazine! That sounded good and would be wonderful promotion of my new book. I immediately gave Jane a copy to take to the editor. Meanwhile, I started my own promotion again. Emails, letters and telephone calls to all and sundry in the media world. This was the third book I had written and published in two years and with each book the work load became more time consuming. In addition to marketing my books and all that that involved, preparing and presenting recipes for photography was a lengthy, and often expensive, business. I was given quite a lot of local publicity for which I was grateful. It kept my name in front of the public and helped me sell my books. I was learning fast and managed on a number of occasions to host photographers and reporters on the same day, but at different times. They mostly knew each other any way and it was like a happy and relaxed meeting of friends. They seemed to enjoy coming to me and always said I was easy to work with and to photograph. After such a day the clearing up took a long time. In the early days I would make lots of preparation, finding the best china and silver, do flower arrangements, launder Mother-in-law's beautiful table linen but nowadays they take me as they find me and props are produced on request!

Shortly after Jane had mentioned YOU magazine, I received a telephone call from one of their reporters. "I've been asked by the Editor of YOU magazine to write a feature about you and your book." We agreed on recipes I might prepare for photography and a day and time for the interview.

Although by now I was used to local reporters and photographers coming to my kitchen this was somehow different. It was a magazine published by a major national newspaper, and a golden opportunity for me to tell my story and promote my recipes countrywide. Nothing must go wrong. As I nervously prepared the chosen recipes the telephone rang. It was the reporter calling to ask, "Would you mind if I bring my dog?" Of course not, I replied, trying to sound as casual and unperturbed as possible. A dog in the kitchen? That was the last thing I wanted! But the choice was not mine. I seem to remember Molly was her name, a lovely Labrador with a shiny black coat. I adored her from the moment she leapt from the car and, as promised by her owner, she was perfectly behaved throughout the day.

Two lovely young photographers arrived and during questions from the reporter, who was also very nice, I was photographed in the kitchen, in the garden, preparing a recipe, planting seedlings in the greenhouse and a very splendid photo was taken of my Strawberry Shortbread. This, having been prepared at the crack of dawn, had collapsed a little but the photographer said it would make a perfect picture, and it did. I had really enjoyed the day, it was such a great experience and I was sorry when they all left, especially Molly who I would have loved to keep.

The reporter said the feature would be two to three pages and it was planned to appear at the beginning of August, adding, "but I cannot say with absolute certainty that it will appear, sometimes a last minute story crops up and the space is given to that. Keep your fingers crossed!" I had decided to tell no one but Nell until the publication of my feature was confirmed. The tension and excitement was almost unbearable so I suggested to Adam that we take a week's holiday and we booked in at a small hotel at Budleigh Salterton.

On our return I checked my emails and amongst them was one from Cork International, subject – "book returns"! This was a devastating blow. 1,500 of the 4,000 books were to be returned from the Sainsbury's distributor. Nell's words came to mind "You're with the big boys now Mummy, be careful." What was I going to do with these?

Where was I going to put them? I could not ask my printer to take so many back into store. I telephoned the sender of the email but was reminded of the terms of sale or return. I was confused that they were returning them so soon when the young buyer had been so confident and positive about sales. I telephoned to speak to her only to hear that she had gone to another department. My brilliant contact was lost and the new buyer was clearly not interested in my book.

A space was cleared in the garage in readiness for the return of the books. For the first time I saw what 1,500 books looked like and I had thousands more in store with James! The van driver was really helpful but he didn't have a sack truck which was needed to transport the boxes along our drive and into the garage. Neighbour Basil came to my aid as ever, with not just a sack truck but a wooden palette on which to stand the returned boxes of books. On leaving, the van driver said, "I spend all my time delivering boxes of books then a few months later returning them – it's crazy!"

As a self-publisher, a one woman band, a small business, call it what you will, I had built up a good relationship with the book distributors and they were always so helpful to me. I remember a particular conversation following a 'returns' email when I was told, "Mo I hate sending these to you because I know you do everything yourself, but if it's any consolation, we send just a few hundred books back to you, we return thousands to the big publishers!" I was beginning to learn about the book trade.

Just before my feature was due to appear in YOU magazine I received a telephone call from The Book People. "We believe you and your summer book are being featured in the magazine, would you like us to handle sales?" I was a little bit hesitant and asked if I could come back to them. I rang Nell. "Yes, I should go for that Mummy," was her advice. During my return telephone call to The Book People we decided all my current titles should be offered, Summer, Kitchen and Christmas. We then discussed discounts. What I offered was immediately snapped up and I wished I had offered less – too late now Mo, but learn from it.

I asked about how many books I might sell. "That's difficult to tell. Sometimes we sell as few as 10, it depends on the subject and the feature." She thought for a moment then said, "Nigella was featured a few months ago, she sold 1,000 books." This made me think I might sell 100 books, perhaps a few more if I was lucky.

Another way I had found of promoting my books was through public speaking. I was speaking to a group of ladies and mentioned that I was shortly to be featured in YOU magazine. At the end of my talk when questions are often asked, one of the group stood up and said, "I used to work for that newspaper. I don't know whether you know but it is the best selling Sunday newspaper, so I think you might sell a few books."

When the magazine arrived I was afraid to open it. It is difficult to explain one's reaction when a newspaper or magazine offers to feature you, especially a national with a high profile. Yes, it is very exciting but it can also be quite a worry. You have no control over their text, you do not know how they will interpret what you have said at the interview and no one had ever let me have sight of a feature before it was published, that is very rarely done. And the photographs, they might be ghastly! I'm terribly vain and dress up like a ham bone for a photo call but the camera never lies! I had ordered many copies from Joyce Ball at the village shop. We had friends staying that weekend and soon the papers were collected and the feature read and I spent the remainder of the day basking in glory. Three pages of splendid text and good photos of self and food! What a difference a feature in a national magazine can make, what a coup for a self-published cook from the Black Country.

Quite early the next morning, Monday, I received my first order by email, then two more orders followed. I kept running into the garden to tell Adam, and ringing Nell and the boys. By the Friday of that first week I had sold 3,000 books! The Book People could hardly believe it, "It's absolutely fantastic," they said. "We can't remember when we last had such a response and sales will continue for months." Some titles were running out and now it was my turn to contact all book distributors who might have unsold copies and ask if they would return them to my printer. As they came in, so they were sent out again, together and the ones stored in my garage, and we still needed to print more *Lazy Cook in the Kitchen*. I eventually sold over 6,000 books from that one feature.

I was overjoyed as you might imagine and my head was

buzzing with the promotion I must arrange following this success. As I looked through the 'best seller' list for that week I noticed the listing of the up and coming young Jamie Oliver having sold 800 or so of one of his books, I had sold 3,000, surely my name should be there? I emailed the data base company who compile that particular list pointing out that my sales were well in excess of the ones listed. Their response was, "We only count the sales that go through a cash till, not mail order sales." How ridiculous I thought, and so typical. But I wasn't proud, I didn't mind how I sold my books.

Dear Pips, Nell's great friend, said I should be featured in *The Bookseller*, a publication I had never heard of. A few telephone calls led me to the person I needed and within a few weeks my summer book was featured. A near half page, with an image of the book, and headed 'Busy times for the enterprising Lazy Cook.' The text began "Nigella Lawson may be publishing *Forever Summer* this week, but she has competition in the shape of Mo Smith......." *The Bookseller* is a trade magazine and the response was staggering. A publisher offered to take over the publication of my books, an Agent offered to promote me quoting a fee of £1,000 – Adam's response was that they should be paying me! Three Dutch publishing companies asked to buy the rights of my books, and booksellers countrywide were ordering copies. There was more to come.

Her practical approach and no-fuss recipes
make cooking seem so simple, but with three
self-published books in two years, Mo Smith
is seriously hard-working for a 'lazy cook'
Report **Sue Carpenter** Photographs **Charlotte Murphy**

Mo's **easy pleasures**

An extract from the feature in YOU magazine, The Mail on
Sunday, 21 July 2002

Busy times for the enterprising 'lazy cook'

Nigella Lawson may be publishing *Forever Summer* (Chatto) this week, but she has competition in the shape of Mo Smith, a 65-year-old, self-published cookery writer. Smith's *A Lazy Cook's Summer: Mouthwatering Recipes for the Time-Pressured Cook* (£6.99, 0954231902) is proving remarkably successful.

The book sold 3,000 copies off-the-page through The Book People after a profile of Smith appeared in the *Mail on Sunday's You* magazine last month. Various outlets have since ordered a further 2,000 copies, the author says. Data from Nielsen BookScan shows the book selling steadily at 50 to 60 copies a week.

A former cookery demonstrator from Bisley in Gloucestershire, Smith began producing her own

A Lazy Cook's Summer

MOUTHWATERING RECIPES
FOR THE TIME-PRESSURED COOK
by Lazy Cook Mo Smith

Self-publishing success

recipe books three years ago, and has negotiated the sale of her titles through Sainsbury and Waitrose supermarkets. Her books, which

include *A Lazy Cook's Christmas* (£4.99, 1929) and *Lazy Cook in the Kitchen* (£6.99, 1910), are also sold in some branches of W H Smith and Ottakar's.

Smith describes herself as "a traditional cook, and a seasonal cook", and says she developed her ideas for dishes that could be cooked quickly when she was nursing her husband through a period of illness and was pressed for time.

Despite the competition from many much glossier cookbooks, this quickfire approach seems to have struck a chord with time-starved readers: "People want good food they can cook at home quickly," the author says.

Trade orders may go to the author on 01452 770298, or e-mail info@lazycookmosmith.co.uk.

Feature from The Bookseller, 6 September 2002

6

I returned home from shopping one day, went into my
emails and amongst them was one from Debbie Nugent at
Thames Television. It read "Dear Mo, I wonder if you
could contact me when you get a chance. I work on a
show called Open House with Gloria Hunniford, which is
a daily afternoon show airing on Channel 5. One of the
regular features is cooking, and on the basis of a recent
article I spotted, I wanted to chat to you about possibly
inviting you along to demo a recipe from your new book. I
would be keen to see a copy of the book also, and would
like to ask to see a copy of it. Perhaps you could let me
know who the publisher is and I could then call in a copy
from them. Please do drop me a line or give me a call
whenever you're free. I look forward to hearing from you
soon, Regards ...."

I couldn't quite believe this! I watched as many cookery
programmes as I was able and often thought, "Oh how I
wish I had the opportunity of demonstrating my recipes on
the television." During that afternoon I returned several
times to this email and read it through again and again. I

didn't mention it to Adam and I didn't even ring Nell, I just pondered on it for the remainder of the day. What it is to be wanted! I eventually made contact with the producer and was invited to attend a recording of the show on Wednesday, 16th October 2002 for transmission the following afternoon. My first concern was, 'what to wear?' I bought a lovely dress but unfortunately it was decided it was too patterned for the cameras and eventually wore black trousers and a top I'd had in my wardrobe for ages. A silk flower, I was told, was the latest fashion trend, and I pinned one on to the top, and Gloria very much admired it. I was given my own dressing room and was chaperoned throughout by Patrice, who gently guided me through the rehearsal and the recording. All the production team was so friendly and the whole atmosphere was relaxing. The producer had chosen some recipes from my book which were cooked for me and most of the time was to be given to Gloria interviewing me about how I had self published and marketed my books. I was just a little disappointed that I wouldn't be showing off my cooking skills, giving tips and presenting my recipes as I wanted them to look, but that was not to be.

Because of the years spent with the BBC I was used to television studios, cameras and lights, none of this phased me at all and on the first run through the studio manager said I was a natural. The one thing that did worry me, and which I mentioned to Patrice, was that once I started to talk about cooking I didn't know when to stop, and time, I knew, would be limited. "Don't worry," said Patrice, "Gloria will handle that," and she did. I didn't actually meet Gloria until the final rehearsal and I was immediately surprised at how tiny she was. Her professionalism put me at ease as we went through the questions she might ask. There was a little preamble about how we would get from the interview and lead into the prepared recipes but that resolved, the scene was set. All the kids turned up. They were all really nervous and were quite amazed at Mother's relaxed performance. The recording was complete and no editing was necessary. Gloria thanked and congratulated me and wished me well. The programme was due to be transmitted the following Monday. Hearing yourself speak over the radio is bad enough but seeing yourself on television is quite horrendous! What a shock! Do I really look like that? Most comments I received were very complimentary and I was congratulated, but on the whole it was said that it was too fast and too rushed and I wasn't given enough time. I received a letter from the series producer thanking me for taking part in the programme, saying how much the team had enjoyed my appearance and hoping I would consider coming on the programme again sometime in the not too distant future. I was pleased that I had made such an impression and very much looked forward to the next time but sadly the programme finished a few months later.

In addition to family and friends and many who I knew had seen the programme, it was viewed by many unknown to me and one such person was Jim McMullan. Jim wrote me an email which I was reluctant to open having recently encountered an expensive computer virus. I didn't recognise the sender's name, should I delete it? Pleased that I hadn't, it read – "Dear Mo, please accept this approach as a compliment. I have just been introduced to your publications by the buyer for a large book group and would be interested to know if you would like representation in the Midlands region" Jim, I was soon to discover, had been involved with the book trade for most of his career working with a well known publisher. He now worked for himself acting as an agent for publishers' lists and asked if I required representation of my titles. He covered a large area of the Midlands and had connections with some 250 outlets. He concluded by wishing me well with my very fine publications. This was like having my eyes opened for the first time on the marketing of books. He also commented on the publication of 'A Lazy Cook's Christmas' saying, it could have been more user-friendly had I used the same typeface as for 'Lazy Cook in the Kitchen'. A bolder and easier type face which would have bulked out the book and the cover price could have been increased by £1.00 without the risk of losing sales. Thank you Mr McMullen, I had only days earlier instructed my printer to print 5,000 more copies of this title!

A few days later I received another email from Jim McMullen – "Dear Mo, I caught your appearance on C5 TV Open House and was impressed. You came over very well indeed and have a natural presence for TV. It was a very professional performance indeed. What was equally important was your voice, clear, friendly, with a most acceptable timbre. You gave the impression you could carry a programme all on your own. Many congratulations. You must be very pleased that this went so well. Regards, Jim."

A further email read, "I sincerely trust that you do not feel that I am taking liberties but I have been working on a better AI for you to consider for a sales aid. What, I wondered is an AI? The email continued, "You may want to change the description and the author profile but this is simply to illustrate lay-out and the limited amount of information you need. It is also to indicate that this is a selling tool and does require to act as a baited hook for the retailer. Have a look and change what you do not like and consider the inclusion of a colour illustration of one of your dishes. I have tested this AI this afternoon and I attach two orders for you. One from W.H.Smith and one from Waterstones, Solihull – 60 books in total. Should you like me to represent you in the Midlands I would be delighted to do this as discussed today. Please advise. Regards, Jim"

Clearly I must meet this Jim McMullen! He was opening the doors to many shops and outlets for my books and his experience in the publishing world was invaluable. Until now I had no idea that publishers had a team of people going round the country selling their latest titles. I had attempted this locally but no way could I venture beyond the Stroud/Gloucestershire area, I didn't have the time or the energy. The complications came when I took a closer look at the AIs I had been sent. These I was soon to learn were Author's Information sheets and each was printed on to a sheet of A4 paper. Setting these up for printing clearly involved computer skills way beyond my ability. The computer screen had to be split down the centre and marked by a line, but not from top to bottom, that might have been simple, but no, first came the heading. Text was then typed on each side of the dividing line, the right hand side text being in double spacing. Finally a photograph of the book, and if available, a photograph of one of my recipes were included. I didn't know where to begin! I didn't feel I could ask Roger Fauske who dealt with all the mechanics of my computer, virus problems, etc. Gerald Parkinson had been such a help but he was a very busy man. The kids were miles away, and on the occasions when they were at home and had time to instruct me on the computer, everything happened at such speed, the screen was constantly changing as they clicked away at the mouse and I was left more confused than ever, unable to remember their teaching. I made copious notes but they didn't make sense the following day. It was, to use an expression of Adam's, like wading through treacle! Then, by a stroke of luck, I met Charlie Walker, recently come to live in the village with his parents who I had known for some time. Charlie was brilliant on the computer and helped me no end; splitting screens, bringing photographs and images of my books on to the screen, then making them smaller or larger and moving them around, even choosing a special type face for the heading. It was all so easy for Charlie and I was so grateful for his help, and remain so. What would have involved me in days of frustration and failure, he did at the click of a mouse – brilliant!

I was by now delighted to let Jim McMullen represent me. Orders came for my books from shops and outlets large and small from all over the Midlands area. Before going to bed I would pack and parcel them up in readiness for posting the next morning. My books were now in many more shops and I was fortunate enough to promote myself into well known West Country and Midlands newspapers and magazines who featured me.

Another email from Jim McMullen arrived. "Would you like to be on Pebble Mill? I have spoken to a Researcher/Broadcast Journalist from BBC Midlands Today about you and she is interested. If I can pull this off she would want to visit your home with an outside broadcast crew and have you do a cookery demonstration in your own kitchen. While there is no guarantee that she will take this further the possibility exists for this to happen pre-Christmas. Can you cope with this? I do recommend that, should this opportunity arise you grab it as Midlands Today is a powerful media." How fortunate I was to have met someone like Jim. His professional expertise his confidence in me and my books and his openness and honesty. My only hope was that I could live up to his expectations!

I could hardly believe it when I was told that a team from BBC Midlands Today would be coming to my kitchen to film five short features to be transmitted on their news each evening in the week running up to Christmas. I was left to choose what to cook and because of the shortage of time, at most two minutes for each recipe, they had to be really quick to make, which suited my Lazy Cook way of cooking. What I didn't realise was that a news presenter would be helping me cook. I could tell immediately that he was unsure of, and doubted my recipes. They were so quick to prepare he didn't believe they would taste good. Timing of course was vitally important and the stopwatch was clicking on and off the whole time. "That took 28 seconds, it must only take 15," said the producer. Cooking instructions had to be limited to a minimum as did the exact words to be spoken whilst the presenter or I was stirring, chopping or decorating a dish. I was glad I was not the only one to get it wrong, sometimes necessitating a retake. It was a long day by the end of which five short Lazy Cook recipes were in the can. Before leaving, the production team tasted my food and immediately became enthusiastic about my recipes and said they would use them over the Christmas period, and beyond. I had lots of telephone calls and messages from long lost friends in the Midlands who had switched on only to be amazed to see Mo! I was later told that the BBC had received a record 1700 hits on their web site requesting my recipes. Quite how many books were sold is difficult to tell. Jim was told that the BBC Midlands TV was interested in another venture in the future but shortly after that our main contact went on sick leave and the plans for an Easter or summer feature went on hold.

LAZY COOK MO SMITH

'LAZY COOK IN THE KITCHEN'
by **Mo Smith**

As featured in the Mail on Sunday YOU
Magazine and in The Bookseller.   As
seen on C5 TV's 'Open House' with
Gloria Hunniford and BBC Midlands
Today.

Last century there was Delia, this
century there is Mo - a cook who
creates recipes for people who want
to assemble a meal in minutes and leave
to cook while they relax in the shower,
with a drink, or in front of the tele.
All Mo's recipes are simple to follow
and are very wholesome and healthy.
Even the most inexperienced cook will
be amazed at the result, how good it
looks and how good it tastes, and the
price is just £6.99 per copy.

Specification

Paperback
ISBN 0954231910
Price £6.99
Size 16.5x23.5cms portrait
Illustrations - line drawings
Available - Jan. 2003

Author Profile edited

Mo Smith's career as a writer began
almost by accident as she was pressed
by her friends for recipes from the
kitchen workshops she ran.
Inundated with enquiries Mo decided
to publish her own book, 'A Lazy
Cook's Chrismas' which rapidly
became a success. From this point
she has now published two further
titles which are creating quite a stir in
the media. The title 'Lazy Cook' fits
the concept of the books although Mo
is anything but lazy having already
marketed her own book to major
supermarkets and, as a result of a
feature in a national newspaper, sold
over 3,000 copies in the first 5 days.
Mo enjoys television and is told that
she is 'a natural' in front of the
cameras. BBC Midlands Today
received over 1700 hits on their
website for Mo's recipes. More
television is in the pipeline. Dec.03

An early Author's Information sheet illustrating my
Savoury Gateau

7

Jim knew the publishing world and the book trade like the back of his hand and from the very beginning had said that my recipe books should be in hard back. In a letter dated January 2003 he wrote, "One thing to consider most seriously, if I may be so bold to suggest a way forward, is to produce an illustrated hardback in time for Christmas 2003. I believe that you are ready to break through to the big time and you will really need to have this kind of publication if you wish to succeed as a cookery writer nationally. You do have the ability and the personality. Now you need national recognition. Your aim should be to have your own TV programme and become the Mrs Beeton of the 21st century. Most of the major names are beginning to pall and folk are looking for a new approach to cooking, a more down to earth approach."

About much of this I couldn't agree with him more, but in reality it was too much for me to contemplate. I had self-published three books in three years, a most exciting and rewarding time, but the work load was increasing as my recipes and my name became better known.

I was now rapidly outgrowing the space I had occupied in the hall for writing. The table which my computer, printer, telephone and everyday papers occupied and my files in boxes around my feet were no longer feasible. I decided to move into a room which until now we had used for storing old unwanted cupboards, a spare refrigerator and general 'junk'. This involved employing builders and suffering all the necessary chaos and disruption until a light and airy new office was completed.

On the domestic front there remained much to do. The home to run, the garden to do especially in the early spring and summer in readiness for Garden Sunday when many visitors came to see it. There was always entertaining to arrange, friends and family staying for weekends, involvement in the village, and neighbours to visit. Also, and not least to consider, was Adam. Following the small stroke a few years earlier he was now unable to drive and needed extra daily care and encouragement. He is the most generous of people in every way and never minds all the time I spend at the computer. He is just so happy for me and so proud when I am featured in the media or receive a big order. His sense of humour makes me laugh and keep things in perspective. Having been at boarding school during the war he eats everything I put in front of him always commenting afterwards, "That was delicious" even though, following his operation he has no sense of taste or smell. I often question him about this saying, "How can you say that when you can't taste or smell it?" His response is always, "I just know it's good from the way you cook it and present it." What greater compliment could a cook wish for?

Amid the extra activity created from Jim's invaluable help and encouragement, I was now planning and creating recipes for my next book as well as continuing my own promotion of my books and myself as a successful self-publisher. Disappointingly, despite all the publicity I had received over the past months through television and a national feature, I continued to receive rejections from many editors in the national media and from newspapers, magazines and radio. Was this because I had self-published my books and they were not taken seriously. I was equally disappointed, and somewhat surprised, when I was refused membership to the Guild of Food Writers. I quote from their letter – "Your strength in the food world is most impressive, but the Committee recommend you try again when you have had more work published by independent publishers. I feel sure they will be delighted to accept you at that stage." "How very strange," I thought. For years my recipes had been published in a magazine, and for many years I had broadcast my recipes on live radio. Whether my recipes were published by myself or a publisher had made no difference to their content and their acceptance by so many members of the public. The attitude of the committee seemed very narrow to me and there appeared an air of snobbery about it. Did all their members have a CV equal to mine? I wondered, albeit they doubtless had a publisher behind them. I could not be bothered to acknowledge the letter although many friends and family were only too anxious to dictate a reply on my behalf! I was happy to send my returned subscription of £70 to charity, and put it all behind me.

Thankfully I continued to make some very valuable

contacts. The Editor of YOU magazine suggested I write to Angela Mason their Associate Editor (Food, Lifestyle and Travel). From my first approach the response from Angela to my request for my recipes to be considered for inclusion in the magazine following their recent feature, was positive and helpful. The following, taken from an email, is an example of this. "By chance I was in the office this morning dealing with some emails and I saw that our food desk had been in touch. I am sorry not to have been able to write to you myself before now – and sorry, too, that we can't be more encouraging as far as recipe features go. As you can imagine, we have to say no to so much material submitted to YOU simply because there isn't room for everything ... if this changes I will let you know. In the meantime, I'd be happy to mention your books on my news page at the front of the magazine. I have everything I need to write the item, I think, but do let me know if you would rather I didn't do so. With very best wishes for your continued success, Yours Angela Mason" What an uplifting email and what a privileged position I found myself in. By chance, this editor had seen my email but had not ignored it, and further added, "I'd be happy to mention your books." A near half page promotion of my three books, with front page images, and the brilliant heading HAVE YOU GOT A MO? appeared in the magazine just a few weeks later resulting in sales of 1,500 books!

I had also been in contact over several months with the distributors to the former Safeway Supermarket chain and one day I heard that they had accepted my Summer book for sale in their stores countrywide. I heard from Waterstone's Head Office, a company I had been targeting for some time. They were also interested in promoting my Summer book in some of their stores. Following many telephone calls and emails regarding quantity, delivery and discounts, I eventually received an order from them – hooray! Yet more excellent promotion of my books! But it turned out to be not quite so straight forward as appeared and on examination of the order I discovered I was expected to pay large discounts not only to Waterstones but also to the distributors, in all totalling over 100%. I didn't need a qualification in accounting to realise I would be paying them to sell my books. After more telephone calls and emails between the three interested parties all was resolved satisfactorily but this brought home to me my lack of business experience. A qualified marketing person would have sorted this from the beginning.

BBC Radio Gloucestershire Producers Anna King and Trish Campbell, continued to come to my kitchen every three weeks or so to record my insert for their afternoon programme. As I talked through the recipe I often wished I could show just how I was preparing and cooking the ingredients. The listeners clearly enjoyed my broadcasts and requested recipe sheets which were now printed on the BBC Radio Gloucestershire website. "Just send them to me by email attachment," said Anna. By an attachment, how do I do that? Anna then very kindly instructed me on how this was done – I was learning all the time!

One morning I answered a telephone call. The voice was very familiar although I could not place it but as the conversation continued I realised, yes, of course, it was a reporter from BBC Points West, the local evening news programme. "We have a camera in the area, could we come and film you cooking something in your kitchen?" "That would be very nice," I said, "when would you like to come?" "When would it suit you?" came the reply. I had a quick think. I had to decide what to cook, possibly shop for the ingredients and get it all prepared. A glance at the clock told me it was 12.50 pm. "Four thirty-ish?" I suggested. "Oh no, that's far too late, can we be with you around 1.30 pm.?" I couldn't turn down such an opportunity, I had to agree to this. I put the telephone down, explained to Adam what was about to happen and quickly thought about what to cook. It was Shrove Tuesday, I knew there would be no point in making pancakes, they had no doubt spent the morning filming pancake races and would have walked out of my kitchen at the very suggestion. I had been experimenting with batter mixtures for my new book and was pleased with my recipe 'Fish in Batter', and which I made with prawns and served with a quick, and very lazy, tomato sauce. This is an excellent recipe to serve as a starter or a way perhaps of encouraging children to eat real fish as opposed to fish fingers. By now it was two minutes to one o-clock. I had all ingredients for the batter but no fish. I ran like the clappers down the hill to the village shop in the hope Joyce Ball would have some. She didn't have a tin, as I would have preferred, but I was lucky enough to buy the last packet from the freezer, I hoped they would be thawed in time for filming, but I had no choice.

Back at home I made the batter mixture, dusted the kitchen shelves, put on a quick face, combed my hair, and was ready and waiting when the film crew arrived. They were so nice and the filming went really well. As is usual, at the end of my demonstration I served fish in batter to the presenter not realising until afterwards that fish was one food he disliked – how to make friends and influence people! Finally I was interviewed about my Lazy cooking and before returning to the studios they went to Waitrose in Stroud and filmed my books on the shelves alongside those of the celebrities. I was told it would be transmitted the following week, they would ring and let me know the particular evening. But what happened? The Iraq war broke out, all projected arrangements were cancelled, my film never saw the light of day.

Emails from Jim continued – "Dear Mo, splendid news about BBC Points West. Very well done indeed. I believe that you need your own series on TV. Have a good holiday and when you return I expect to have some exciting news for you. Jim." The news came as part of another email, as follows – "now for my good news. I have been quiet, but not idle. There is a distinct possibility that I can negotiate a deal with a major publisher. Seriously. This is now on the cards so it is time to discuss what you want and which direction you wish to take." Some weeks later I met Jim on Paddington Station as we had arranged and we made our way by tube to the publishing house to meet the Publishing Director. She reported that they were very enthusiastic about my books and they would like to publish a collection of my recipes, gleaned from my various books, under the title The Lazy Cook. They would publish the book in hardback in autumn 2004 (it was now the summer of 2003). It would be medium format sized, with colour photographs throughout. They would be responsible for the photography, though they would want me to be involved to ensure that the pictures had the right 'feel' I was after. They would actively promote me with a marketing and publicity campaign at publication, but also would seek to raise my profile in the run up to publication. They had already spoken with the commissioning editor for food programming on UK food and had many more contacts. They proposed an initial print run of around 12,000 copies with the facility to reprint quickly. Royalties were discussed with Jim whose professional knowledge came to the fore and, in the nicest way, he was prepared to argue for the best deal. I just listened. I was asked what I was willing to do by way of promotion, travelling to signings etc. These tours would be limited to the areas where TV coverage could be gained, such as London, Bristol, Cardiff, Manchester, Leeds, Newcastle, Glasgow, Edinburgh and Birmingham. I could hardly believe this was real? I thought I must be dreaming! It was one of the most exciting things that had happened to me, not just anyone, but a large publisher was offering to publish my recipes – wow! I also secretly wondered who would look after Adam while I was swanning around the countryside signing books!

Shortly after our meeting a contract was received. Jim had a few points he wished to clear up otherwise he thought, as a new author, I was getting a good deal. In the meantime more interest in my books came from the Marketing Director of another publishing company asking Jim if she could keep the copy of my book *A Lazy Cook's Summer* as she was so impressed with it. She said that she would keep it on her office bookshelf and would promote it whenever she had media people in her office. This sudden enthusiasm and interest in my books started to go to my head and when I heard from Jim that this large publishing conglomerate was very keen on my books and wanted to publish a compendium of my recipes, I couldn't resist the temptation to meet them. I now realise that this put Jim in a very difficult position and he was having to play for time with the other publishers who were pressing for completion of their contract. At the beginning of our meeting with the second interested publisher, we learnt that the director of the publishers who had offered me a contract, had suddenly and surprisingly walked out of her job. And so this meeting which had been arranged as an introduction to The Lazy Cook was turned about, and we were now discussing the possibility of them publishing my recipes. The meeting was relaxed and appeared to go very well and at one point the interviewer congratulated me on my marketing ability and said that she knew celebrity writers who would be envious of the publicity I had achieved for myself. In a follow up letter Jim thanked her for the kind hospitality, for the time allowed and for the professional consideration of my work. He wanted her to know that I felt very comfortable about the ideas put forward and had expressed a desire to move further down the road toward having talks on the possibility of joining them.

Meanwhile, in view of the unexpected resignation, the unsigned contract went on hold until a new publishing director was appointed, which could take several months. Even so they were still very keen to complete and publish my recipes and the Editorial Manager wrote to Jim – "I'll get back to you and Mo with a firm offer as soon as the newly appointed Publishing Director starts in

November. We decided it was a bit unfair to present her with a fait-accompli list so we're holding off on all contracting until she starts. I really think this will be a great book for our list and we look forward to working with you on this." But the new Publishing Director did not think so and wrote to Jim – "This project looks very interesting in itself and Mo is obviously a fascinating and engaging cook and I am sure the books will be very publishable, but I am afraid that they do not quite fit the profile that I foresee for us in the immediate future." An equally disappointing response came from the publishing conglomerate, a part of which Jim read to me over the telephone – "I am terribly sorry to be writing to say that, after some debate and careful consideration, we have decided not to pursue this any further. I am very disappointed because I enjoyed meeting Mo immensely. She is a great personality and her determination has clearly struck a major chord with many aspiring cooks". In a final confirmation of this by email Jim concluded ... "do not be disheartened as you have something very valuable within and many, many authors have gone through what you must be experiencing at present. If at first we don't succeed try, try and try again. Our aim now is to make both publishers quite ill with envy of the publisher that takes you on. There can be only one winner – Mo Smith – Lazy Cook. My very best wishes to an extraordinary cook. Jim."

It would have been fibbing to say I was not gutted by this news and I blamed myself for not signing the contract – a bird in the hand and all that! I was disappointed also for Jim who had worked so hard on my behalf.

After a period of time I began to ask myself, "Do I really want a publisher?" I've done very nicely thank you with my current books, why hand all this over and in doing so lose the kudos of being, as I am constantly reminded, one of the most successful self-publishers? O.K. so I don't have pictures in my books, so what? No one has ever said, "There are no photographs of your dishes in your books". On the contrary most readers prefer to have no pictures. "Your recipes are so easy to follow, pictures date the food, your recipes are timeless," I was often told.

Sometimes I receive telephone calls from authors asking for advice on self-publishing. Have I started a trend? But there are also the downsides, the endless hours spent marketing your work, the financial risk and, at the end of it all you may not sell one copy. It is also a very solitary occupation. I was interested recently to read a feature on self-publishing in the Society of Authors publication (Winter 2004). One author had written "I had self-published back in the 1990s and I was determined that I was not going to totally self-publish again because it is one of the most crushing things to do. You have to have tremendous faith in your work and keep pushing, pushing, pushing. I don't want to be so alone again." I knew that feeling only too well.

Encouraged by the family, at the beginning of January 2004 I started work on my fourth book – *The Lazy Cook's Favourite Food*. I had planned that this would be slightly bigger than my previous titles and in addition to the recipes under the usual headings, it would also include advice on healthy eating, cooking for one, and information and recipes for children under the heading 'Grandma, can we make some cakes?' By sheer coincidence, two of these topics, healthy eating and children's food, were at the forefront of the news and celebrity writers were filling our screens and newspapers with their recipes and solutions to the serious problem of obesity which was affecting not merely the health but also the behaviour of many people of all ages. This assured me that my new lazier than ever, healthy recipes would be topical.

I chose purple as the cover colour and decided to approach editors of magazines who had featured me and ask if I could use a quote from them and their name as part of the back cover. First amongst these was Angela Mason at YOU Magazine who agreed to my request but stipulated the removal of the 's' from the word 'magazines'. I passed this on to my cover designer who later confirmed that he had made the alteration. The decision as to how many books to have printed was a difficult one, there were so many new cookery writers coming on to the market since I began and even more television programmes. Even so I had a good following and interest from some branches of the media remained positive. Earlier in the year I had received a message from Angela Mason at YOU magazine saying, "By all means let us know later in the year when your new book is published. I'll be very happy to mention you on my Food News page." Ottakar's had recently opened a new store in Cheltenham and they asked if I would like them to launch my new title. This was further confirmation that my books were recognised by the book trade who were volunteering promotion such as I had never imagined. It was now mid-September, once again I was well past my proposed deadline and it was already getting late for the Christmas trade and possible features. In view of this James and I decided to print 3,500 copies only, and more could be printed as needed.

HAVE YOU GOT A MO?

Mo Smith's *Lazy Cook* books have been unexpectedly solid sellers since YOU first told their story last year. Unexpectedly, because Mo, who is in her 60s, wrote the first (*A Lazy Cook's Christmas*) to sell to friends and acquaintances, based it on her cookery demos and rapid-response hostessing at home in Gloucestershire, and self-published it utterly unadorned (nobody's seen a cook book *sans* glossy pix for decades – it had shock value). There followed two more – *Lazy Cook in the Kitchen* and *A Lazy Cook's Summer* – printed in bigger quantities and determinedly self-marketed, until Waitrose and Sainsbury's came calling. The audience out there responded to her candid titles and her family cheese pie or baked bean pie recipes (as well as more modern-sounding goodies). Fans will have to wait a year for Mo's next book, due autumn 2004; meanwhile, here's another chance to buy Mo's books via the YOU Bookshop. To order your copy of *A Lazy Cook's Summer* (£6.99), *Lazy Cook in the Kitchen* (£6.99) or *A Lazy Cook's Christmas* (£4.99) – or all three for the special price of £15.97 – call the YOU Bookshop on 0870 162 5006, visit the website (www.you-bookshop.co.uk), or send a cheque, made payable to YOU Bookshop, to YOU Bookshop, Unit 17, St James's Court, Warrington WA4 6PS. Prices include delivery.

Feature from YOU magazine, The Mail on Sunday, 31 August 2003

As I had experienced in the past, the best laid plans do not always work out. Having left all printing matters in the capable hands of James, suitcases were packed and my sister Audrey and brother-in-law Freddie arrived to spend another holiday together. This time in an apartment belonging to friends Jane and Norman at Thurlestone, Devon. We were concerned as to whether Freddie, now having difficulty walking, would manage our spiral staircase. We were leaving the following morning. Freddie walked up our staircase almost like a two year old, but later that evening Adam came tumbling down. I was brushing my teeth in the bathroom when I heard such a resounding crash, then absolute silence. Rushing to the stairs I saw Adam in a heap at the bottom of the stairs. He had crashed into a vase which was now in smithereens. Time seemed to stand still. It was terrifying. For a moment I thought he was dead, until suddenly he began to groan. It was such a frightening scene, lots of blood and the groaning was awful. I dialled 999 for an ambulance then, not for the first time when in need of help, I rang Miriam Frings our lovely friend and neighbour. She and husband Pete were wonderful and Miriam being a nurse was able to make Adam a little more comfortable and advised me to get a blanket to keep him warm until the paramedics arrived. Miriam insisted on driving me behind the ambulance to Stroud hospital from where, after examination he was transferred to Gloucester Royal. Again Miriam insisted on driving me, her support and professional help was calming and invaluable.

Adam was in hospital for over two weeks. Audrey and Freddie stayed with me and their presence and a ready prepared meal when I arrived home from hospital visits was marvellous. During this stay in hospital Adam became weak and confused and I just wanted to get him home, even though he needed the assistance of a wheelchair. The hospital staff kept asking me, "How will you cope?" How would I cope? The same as I've always coped, what difference would there be? But it was different. Adam needed round the clock t.l.c. – and I had thousands of books to sell! But there was more to come. James had agreed to perfect bind 300 or so copies of the books in readiness for the launch and on the preceding Friday afternoon, just a few days after Adam's return home, I collected a handful of these copies. We had a village event planned for that evening which I was able to attend while Keith Rogers sat with Adam. Before going to bed I took the first real look at my new book. I was pleased with the overall appearance of the front cover but on glancing at the back page the first thing I noticed was the misprint of the YOU magazine wording! The 's' from magazines had not been deleted. I could not believe my eyes! I was devastated. I had given my word to Angela Mason at YOU that this would be corrected and had received confirmation that the alteration had been made – what had gone wrong? I concluded that there was nothing I could do at that moment. James would be closed for the weekend but first thing on Monday morning I must contact him. I put a large note alongside my bed reminding me to set the alarm in time to speak to James by 8-o-clock the following Monday morning to ask if he could correct this mistake. But I was too late, he had gone into work on the Saturday morning to complete my promised order. I could hardly believe my misfortune. Why had I not tried to ring him on the Saturday morning?

Somewhere along the line there had been a mix up but there was only one person to blame, myself, I should have checked more carefully. On reflection I realised that I should have requested James to scrap them and reprint the corrected cover.

The proposed book launch about which I had been so excited, paled into insignificance. I was unable to find anyone to sit with Adam that evening so I had no option but to leave him in the house alone. It was lovely to be supported at the launch by so many friends some of whom, like Stella, had travelled from afar on that cold, wet and windy evening. I attempted a few words of thanks to them all but suddenly I was overcome with emotion and our dear Ed, the only one of the children who had been able to attend, came to my rescue. Friends Bobbie and Gerald offered to return home to be with Adam so that I could take Ed and his friends Nathan and Antonia out for a celebratory meal.

For many weeks I was fearful of leaving Adam alone for long and I was grateful to many friends and neighbours who gave me much help and support. Very soon I had a list of 'sitters'. All promotion and last minute publicity of my new book was now secondary in my thoughts and for the time being would have to be abandoned. Would I ever find time, or stamina, to attempt this and catch the Christmas market?

But all was not lost and help came from Nicky Rogers who, with husband Keith and son Tom, had recently come to the village and lived in the house we had left to come to

BOOK LAUNCH

Lazy Cook Mo Smith

is pleased to invite you to the launch of her new book

'The Lazy Cook's Favourite Food'

on

Wednesday, 20th October

6.00p.m. - 7.30p.m.

at

Ottakar's, The Promenade, Cheltenham

Bear House. Nicky had taken over all my clerical work, postage and packing, she was the most efficient and caring assistant I could wish to find. She posted copies of my new book to the many contacts I had in the media. I now had a good database of names and addresses of many who had bought my books over the years and Nicky sent a mailshot to these announcing my new book, the response was good and many copies were sold. But sales through book chains and supermarkets were vitally important and my hopes of such sales were further dashed when the buyer I had negotiated sales with at Waitrose left and the new buyer turned down *The Lazy Cook's Favourite Food*. The market was changing so rapidly. There were so many new books being printed, many covering special themes such as Dieting and Healthy Eating. Titles such as 'Simple meals', 'Meals in Moments', 'Easy Cooking' appeared – all very much on the lines of 'Lazy' cooking but they all had photographs, and publishers and their teams of marketing expertise.

The fact that I had sent a book with the misprint on the back cover to Angela Mason at YOU magazine, with whom I had built up such a good contact, played on my mind and I decided I must write offering my sincere apologies for this error, and for not keeping my word. I did not know at the time of writing how this mistake had occurred but I acknowledged that at the end of the day the responsibility lay with me. I assured her that this would be corrected on the next print run. In conclusion I repeated how very much I valued their promotion of my books. I felt the thousands of readers who had ordered my books through their magazine in the past would welcome this new book and I hoped this would not affect any promotion they might be considering of this my latest book. Angela replied, "Dear Mo. Thanks for explaining what happened. As it stands the book arrived too late to be mentioned pre-Christmas anyway (we're working on New Year issues now). If I can mention it at some point in the future, I'll let you know, of course. best wishes. AM."

My changed personal circumstances and the support and encouragement I needed to give to Adam, limited the time I could spend marketing my new book. I did what I could, when I could, but I lost out on the important months of media and retail Christmas sales promotion.

9

As we entered the year 2005 the words of my late Mother-in-law repeatedly came into my mind, "you give yourself so much work dear." I felt drained, and the last thing I wanted was to restart promotion of my book. So I didn't. They were only paper after all, they could wait, something much more important was on the horizon – Nell and Robin planned to marry in May which also happened to be the year and month of our 40th wedding anniversary. People so often said, marrying off a daughter is the most stressful thing you can do. I didn't want it to be stressful. Nell is so dear to us, as are Ed. and Bill and we were all so happy that she was marrying Robin. I wanted to enjoy every moment of it, helping to make all the arrangements, as well as the day itself. I forgot book promotion, and con-centrated on the wedding of the year, and our own anniversary celebration – and what a happy and memo-rable weekend it was – absolutely wonderful!

Before very long my fingers were itching to get back to the computer and pick up on marketing my latest book but this had not got any easier. Everybody, it seems, was writing about cooking and with increased coverage on the television the market was flooded with new cookery books. Retail outlets and the media are now only interested in new titles, anything a few months old is not considered, and my latest book was 8 months old.

In conversation one day with the daughter of a friend who was following a career in publishing, Lizzie Curtin said, "I've been thinking of your books Mo and a way of marketing them might be to write to some of the editors of the many house and antiques magazines. You have a lovely house and garden and I think it would make a great feature." I wrote to one such magazine, intending to write to many more, but allowed myself to be put off by this first rejection.

I followed up approaches I had previously made to the BBC *Good Food* magazine. As a regular contributor to BBC Radio Gloucestershire I thought they might take some of my recipes but the response was, as before, we only feature celebrity chefs from Ready-Steady-Cook and similar television programmes. I tried to make contact with the editor of BBC Points West, Woman's Hour, Midweek, The Food Programme and others, but without response.

Clearly, the Lazy Cook had to think of a new approach to marketing her recipes. It was now the beginning of summer 2005. Schools would soon be breaking up for the long summer holidays. Mums and Grannies, Uncle Tom Cobbly and all might be pondering what to do with these little darlings over this period of many weeks. I decided this could be as good a time as any to introduce them to cooking and compiled the following feature.

Entertaining the kids on rainy days

With the advent of another long summer holiday many parents will be at a loss to know how to entertain the kids, without spending a fortune, especially on rainy days. My Lazy Cook recipes are quick and easy, creative and fun to make; they encourage healthy eating and can be enjoyed by all the family.

As a cook, I can think of no better way of bonding with children, whether as a parent or a grandparent, than introducing them to cooking – getting them away from the telly and into the kitchen. When little fingers set to work on the flour and fat the concentration is a joy to behold even though the tasting can be something else!

Make a batch of choux paste (as easy as making custard). Let the kids spoon it out on to baking trays then sit them in front of the oven to watch them rise and cook – (so much better than watching telly). Fill them with savoury or sweet fillings (the pastry, not the children!) then all sit round the table and eat and giggle together.

I also remembered a conversation I had had after the wedding breakfast with Mags, the wife of Robin's Best Man. She questioned me about my books and was most interested to hear about how I had published and marketed them myself. She was just setting up as a freelance marketing consultant and said how she would love the opportunity of marketing my books. She had two toddlers and was finding it really difficult to find time to cook healthy evening meals, and when entertaining. She did not want to buy ready made meals. "I want to make the kind of meals my Mother and Gran cooked," she said, "not expensive and fancy, just good home cooking, everyday meals that everybody can enjoy and the preparation of which does not take hours and leaves me exhausted." She continued, "There are thousands of mums out there who are in a similar position to myself. Have you heard of the parents magazines now on sale. There are two I know of, 'Families' and 'Angels and Urchins', your recipes would be perfect for their readers, I will send you copies."

I decided to offer the 'Entertaining the kids.....' feature to the editors of each of these magazines but with the addition of the following paragraph which I felt would be of further interest to young parents –

"I also enclose a potted history of my background outlining the progress I have made as a self-publisher into the very competitive cookery book market. This I feel sure would be of interest to young people who feel cut off from careers they once enjoyed before parenthood, and an incentive to them to continue their skills from home, taking advantage of the many opportunities offered through the media of computers and modern technology."

I should have realised their summer copy would by now have gone to press but I am still in touch with the editor of 'Families' and there is the possibility of a feature in the future.

Meanwhile, I emailed this 'Entertaining the kids.....' feature in the form of a press release to a number of newspapers and received immediate interest from the *Bristol Evening Post*, and the national newspaper, *Weekly News* – I was back in business!

I had learnt long ago that you cannot rest on your laurels. I needed to keep pushing myself, my recipes and my books, but how was I to do this and be noticed? The idea came to me while I was gardening, as so often happens. I would take a break from promotion of my books and concentrate on promoting individual recipes. I planned to send these by press release on the first day of each month, under the heading 'The Lazy Cook's Tip of the Month'. To present these in a more original form and one which might catch the eye of editors, I wrote them beginning with opening chat about a particular ingredient then talked through a recipe using the chosen ingredient. The following, (my Christmas 2005 press release) illustrates more clearly the theme of these features.

Double Cream

Always buy double cream – it will keep fresh much longer; it can be made into single cream by stirring in a little milk; it will thicken a sauce and, should you overbuy, a 10oz carton can be whipped and used to line a 2pt basin and then frozen in readiness to make into The Lazy Cook's Chocolate Bomb – a superb pudding to delight family and friends.

CHOCOLATE BOMB – *serves 6–8 portions*
Whip a 10oz. carton of double cream to a spreadable consistency, stir in 3–4 teas. ready grated chocolate then spread to cover the inside of a 2pt. basin, put into a freezer bag and freeze. Make the filling by melting 100g. bitter chocolate with

50g butter, stir in 4 egg yolks (using large sized eggs), and 50g chopped walnuts (optional). Using a large bowl, whisk the egg whites to a stiff consistency then stir in the chocolate mixture. Pour into the frozen cream mould, put back into the freezer bag and freeze for a minimum of 24hrs. or until required. To serve, remove the freezer bag and put the bomb into a refrigerator to thaw a little before loosening the side with a palette knife and turn on to a serving dish. Leave in a refrigerator to continue to thaw for 3–4hrs. or until the centre has defrosted (test with a metal skewer). Before serving, spike with chocolate squares, or for a more dramatic presentation, spike sparklers in the top and light.

At the end of the day it was all focused on selling my books and the features ended with details of a special reader offer. Again Nell gave me good advice, "Don't offer them all in the first feature, just offer one title, say, for the next two months, or until stocks last, and change it from time to time" – how easy it is when you know how!

I was encouraged when the first of these was accepted by Bill McBride, a contact I had made with the *Weekly News*. "The editor seems to like your recipes and has agreed to feature these each month," said Bill. At this point Nell further advised me, "Mummy, you must ask which week will they appear in and the copy deadline date. Specify, that you will choose the subject each month. Request that a photograph of yourself appears alongside each feature; also that a copy of each edition be sent to you for your file; and ask that each feature ends with a special reader offer and your website." After putting these questions to Bill during a telephone call, I was amused when he said,

"You've obviously done this many times before, I'm very impressed!"

Another welcome acceptance came from Joe Pontin of the *Bristol Evening Post*. They would feature my recipes in their 'Severn' magazine to run each week between November and Christmas and, at my request, their photographer Clint Randall could take the photographs. Clint had photographed me many times in the past for their *Country Life* magazine and I looked forward to his return visit to my kitchen.

So often, when you think everyone has forgotten you, the telephone will ring. This happened when a new young features writer with the *Gloucestershire Echo* telephoned one day and said she would like to feature me. I had for many years hoped I might be featured in their 'Weekend' magazine and now was my opportunity. Unable to spare the time to visit me before the copy deadline date, the interview was conducted over the telephone. As I have mentioned before, although an exciting prospect at the time, features don't always turn out to be quite as you might imagine, or hope for. But I'm sure this young writer has a great future in journalism, she wrote a great feature. Across two pages was the heading "If you're short of time, 'Lazy Cook' Mo Smith has recipes for kitchen success – she can make meals in a Mo-ment." It continued ... "no chef is worth their salt unless they have a television series, restaurant chain and a political crusade. But self-proclaimed Lazy Cook Mo Smith is a different kettle of fish. Emma Race spoke to the queen of laid-back meals."

Katie Jarvis, Chief Writer, for the popular *Cotswold Life* magazine had for many years been an admirer of my work and from time to time featured my recipes. She continued my promotion with a 'Cotswold Character' feature.

My Christmas Press Release was picked up by Anna Trapmore, Commissioning Editor of the *Sunday Express* 'S' magazine who promoted my book 'A Lazy Cook's Christmas' under the Books for Cooks section. All this exposure kept my name in front of the public – yes, I think I could say with confidence that I was back in business.

"Kindly do not use your mobile" is requested by Mills Café in Withey's Yard, Stroud, but our friend Angela Robinson who runs a bed and breakfast and who we meet regularly on a Wednesday morning, occasionally receives a call. This prompted me one morning to check my mobile, there was an unidentifiable symbol in one corner. "You have a message," said Angela and showed me how to receive it. It was from someone called Kate Atkinson at ITV Central News asking if I would call her back. Kate had also picked up my press release and asked if I would travel to their studio at Abingdon, Oxfordshire to be interviewed for their mid-day news. I felt Kate was a little taken aback when she saw that I was not in the prime of youth, but the luscious pudding (a Chocolate Bomb), and the chocolates I had taken in soon won her over, and the remainder of the news team. The interview was recorded in one take. No editing was needed and it was transmitted in that lunchtime news programme. I was invited to stay behind to watch and reluctantly accepted partly because we could not get this news channel at home, although I had asked friends to record it for me. I had not put on special make-up and hadn't even combed my hair for the recording – what a sight I looked! However, the content of the interview seemed to go down well with the viewers and I was telephoned a few days later asking if they could film me cooking a turkey. Just days later a reporter and cameraman arrived at Bear House. As it was for a news insert a maximum of two minutes was allowed – not a long time to cook a turkey and the trimmings and give handy hints, concentrate on what you are doing, and saying, and remember to smile – a tall order you might say! But they did a splendid job. The reporter was happy to stay out of the picture and let me get on with it. The cameraman said I was so relaxed and natural I should have my own programme. "To film this with one of the celebrities would take at least a day and several cameras, and I guarantee it wouldn't be any better than this, if as good!" By now I was brimming with pride.

Promotion in the Sunday Express 'S' magazine, December 2005

10

January 2006 and I am nearing my 69th birthday. Time perhaps to retire, to sit back, read more books, watch more television (and criticise all the cookery programmes!) Spend more time in the garden, more time visiting friends and neighbours, perhaps set up my sewing machine and design clothes, make new cushions and curtains, do a little housework! Bear House, I'm sure, feels deprived of the lack of tender loving care it once received from Annie Stevens who helped me for many years and became a friend, a member of the family.

My heart told me that I should give more time to Adam, take him out and about more, have more holidays. Many of our friends and most people of our generation seem to spend more time on holiday than at home. But we're not really holiday people. We love going to Rock in Cornwall, it's home from home. We love the holidays we've had with sister Elsie and Michael at their apartment in Sandbanks. We adore the holidays we've spent with the kids and their spouses, all of us together, Ed and Esme, Will and Lynn, Nell and Robin, sauntering around the winding streets of favourite Italian towns, sitting at pavement cafes and soaking up the atmosphere. Visiting museums and street markets in Paris and finding a nice restaurant for an evening meal, and laughing, yes, doing such a lot of laughing. Yes, it's wonderful but we are always pleased to return home, that lovely old Cotswold house and garden, our peaceful haven.

And so I think again, should I retire from cooking and writing? No, a very definite no echoes from each of the children, you must carry on with your writing Mum. But about what shall I write? Promoting and marketing my cookery books has taken over so much of my life and I have even less time for cooking than ever and doubt I would have enough new recipes to fill another cookery book.

January, February and March come and go. Midway through April I start to write this book and give myself until the end of May to complete the text. It is now 30th May, I'm almost there, whether I will ever publish it is still to be decided. Will I have the energy and the enthusiasm to start marketing and promoting all over again? Will people really want to read it?

During these negative thoughts I remembered the silent concentration with which my talks are received, I remembered a recent talk I gave to a local W.I. meeting at the end of which the very generous vote of thanks concluded, "Your story would be an inspiration to many of today's young people who fear failure and lack confidence to pick themselves up and have a go." Before leaving, a member came up to me and said, "Thank you. Your talk was amazing, so interesting, the best talk I have ever heard, you could have heard a pin drop. I do congratulate you and I do hope you will write your story, I'm sure everyone would love it." I was touched by such genuine praise.

And what about the purple spoon? Well, it became a family joke. As each of the children left home and set up in a flat, amongst the box of kitchen utensils handed down from Mother was the purple spoon. Bill took it to his Edinburgh flat where he was at that time Restaurant Manager of the No.1 Restaurant at The Balmoral Hotel. Bill and Lynn now live in London, where he and his business partner, Antony Demetre, a critically acclaimed chef, have recently opened 'Arbutus', a restaurant in London's Soho. Ed took the purple spoon to his first house in Buckingham. Having given up his job with a Formula 1 racing team he did a degree in Mechanical Engineering and is now a Design Engineer with Palmer Sports. He has a lovely girlfriend, Esme. Nell, who, after getting a degree in Accountancy and Law, found herself in marketing. She and Robin are also still in London and Nell is just setting up her own company – Ruby Shoes Marketing. She called me one evening to say, "Mummy I have something awful to tell you … I dropped the purple spoon and broke its handle off!" And so after many years of constant use it is now wrapped in tissue paper and stored in a box – thank you Francie for the many memories it has brought back to me.

End

Features

The following pages give examples of features I wrote and which I refer to in my story. Some I wrote and were published in the *Gloucestershire and Avon Life* magazine, others I wrote and sent to magazine and newspaper editors.

GLOUCESTERSHIRE & AVON LIFE

WHAT'S COOKING

Mo Smith: Yes, why not lamb?

Mo Smith, the Bisley-based food expert, joins our team this month with the first of a series of topical kitchen comments.

PROMINENTLY displayed in my butcher's shop last week was a notice which read: "why not order new season's lamb for the weekend?" Why not indeed? Instantly my digestive juices started to flow at the thought of roast spring lamb and mint sauce – I have a little early mint in the green-house – new potatoes and peas. What better culinary welcome to a new season?

Modern farming, and progress made over the past decade in the safer storage and preservation of food, have made it possible for us to buy all varieties of meat and poultry at any time of the year. Gone are the days when pork was eaten only when there was an "R" in the month, and turkey was reserved for Christmas. Gone also is mutton, and the many wholesome dishes this gave us, boiled mutton and parsley sauce for instance, or individ-

ual mutton pies to be eaten hot or cold. Indeed, many people still consider mutton the finest and tastiest of all meats.

Lamb contains more fat both around the joints and embedded in the meat, and a fair proportion of bone. Shoulder of lamb is a good example of this, and is often considered a wasteful joint, though a certain amount of fat adds both to flavour and appearance. Food, like fashion, however, has its crazes, and this excess fat and bone, plus the all-year availability of other meats, has cost lamb much of its popularity.

Even so, it still has many points in its favour, new season's lamb in particular. This can easily be recognised by its creamy white fat and bluish tinge in the shoulder knuckle bone. I can think of more ways of preparing and serving any cut of lamb, prime joint or offal, than any other meat. Consider the splendid entré crown of lamb, simplicity itself to prepare and cook and truly magnificent in appearance. In contrast come lamb's kidneys, by no means an inferior addition to a restaurant menu, and usually served in a rich sauce. It is difficult to imagine pigs' or ox kidneys, presented in this way, having similar appeal.

Before introducing one of my favourite recipes, let me pass on a few hints for preparing, cooking and serving lamb. I referred earlier to the amount of fat contained in a lamb joint. It is better to remove all excess fat and render it down for dripping than for it to be left on the side of a plate and wasted. Similarly, the bone can be removed from a shoulder joint; a butcher will do this, given a few days' notice.

The cavity can be filled with a farce or stuffing to your own liking, adding extra flavour, colour and texture to the joint and easing the carver's chore. An additional bonus, and an important one is that the joint will go further.

A joint which has been frozen for too long might be slightly strong in flavour. A few slices of fresh garlic inserted into the joint before cooking will tenderise the meat and add a subtle flavour. Rosemary is another herb which complements lamb. Tuck a few fresh sprigs around the joint before cooking.

Finally, here is my recipe for lamb cutlets to serve hot or cold. They can be included in a summer picnic or in a more sophisticated hamper for the coming Badminton weekend.

Allow two cutlets per adult. Buy them in a piece, best end or loin, and ask the butcher to "chine" them, stopping him before he chops two inches from the rib-bone, shortening the stick. Using a sharp knife, divide the joint into individual cutlets. Cut away all the meat and fat two inches down the rib-bone and trim off any excess fat further down the cutlet. This can all be rendered down.

Flatten each cutlet with a kitchen mallet or wooden rolling pin and coat first in beaten egg with a little salt added, then a mixture of fresh breadcrumbs and finely chopped cooked ham, pressing it well into each cutlet. Fry the cutlets in a little hot dripping for about three minutes on each side. The outside should be crisp, and the inside slightly pink.

Dry on kitchen paper and pop a cutlet frill on each stick before serving. These can be prepared several days in advance and kept in a fridge until required for cooking – or they can be frozen, uncooked, until needed. Serve them with a piquant tomato sauce.

April 1983

My first feature for the Gloucestershire & Avon Life magazine

GLOUCESTERSHIRE & AVON LIFE

ELIZABETH DAVID, holidays abroad, and television have each played their part in introducing us to the delights of French cuisine. As a consequence there are many restaurants in this country serving traditional French dishes and nouvelle cuisine. Among these is Le Champignon Sauvage, a newly opened French restaurant in Suffolk Road, Cheltenham.

Our evening began in a warm and comfortable room adjoining the restaurant and from the bar we were served drinks with a selection of mouth-watering homemade savouries. The menu, written in French but with English translations, offered a first and main course for £12.95 per person. From a wide choice Sally ordered breast of pigeon and a sea-bass roast and I chose a *ragôut* of mussels and medallions of venison. After consultation with the waiter and a sample tasting of the house wines, we decided these would be good with the dishes we had selected. I ordered a glass of red Cuvée Parisot with my venison and Sally requested Cuvée Parisot Blanc with her fish. They proved excellent choices.

In the dining room our table was set with linen of delicate shades of pink and grey to match the décor throughout the restaurant. A small candle was lit and warm homemade rolls were offered. My first course consisted of fresh mussels, bacon pieces and new-season's chestnuts served in a rich cream sauce. A few mussel shells had been carefully placed among the ingredients adding a touch of perfection to the presentation of this very colourful first course which was delicious.

Sally was equally complimentary about her first course. The pigeon breast had been carefully sliced and reshaped to form a fan and this was surrounded by a contrasting sauce. A parcel of bright cabbage leaves and bacon, described as a casserole of cabbage and bacon, completed the dish giving additional flavours and colour to this excellent course.

The presentation of my main course was equally dramatic. Slices of venison, cooked pink, were arranged in the centre of the plate and a half pear, poached to a dark rich colour, stood majestically alongside. Dainty portions of vegetbles surrounded these two ingredients, including carrots, haricots verts, calabrese and a potato gratinée. A pear liqueur sauce completed the dish. It was a superb course, rich in flavour, colour and texture.

Continued

Sally's portion of sea bass was topped with a large fresh prawn and surrounded with a salsify sauce and more, smaller prawns. In complete contrast to the fish the sauce was very dark in colour and the flavour was a little rich for her palate. Even so she enjoyed the fine flavours of the fish and the accompanying vegetables which were also included.

After two very excellent and satisfying courses we wondered if we could do justice to a dessert. However, one look at the menu changed all that and during the short interval between courses we quietly anticipated the arrival of the dessert which we knew would be good – we were not disappointed. In the centre of my plate a slice of cream almond mousse was placed. Included in this mousse were pieces of tropical fruits which sat like jewels in velvet. Neat arrangements of many different fruits encircled the centrepiece – strawberries, mango, kiwi and passion fruit. Raspberries and clusters of berries of different colours and flavours and over all these a bright fruit sauce was trailed. The combined flavours were sharp, fresh and delicious.

The iced praline Sally had selected was similarly presented. A cream caramel sauce surrounded the ice and into this sauce fresh stawberries had been set. It was a fine assortment of good flavours which Sally enjoyed immensely.

Coffee and homemade petits fours completed our meal the total cost of which was £41.15 including VAT but excluding service.

After our meal I was able to meet David Everitt-Matthias, chef and joint owner of Le Champignon Sauvage, with his wife Helen, who is the manageress. In response to our congratuations David was anxious to emphasise that the standard set at the restaurant was only possible with the co-operation of his team which includes his wife, David Offley the second chef and Alex Lawrence the head waiter. In David's own words, "we are only as good as they are."

It was refreshing to meet so young a British chef with such talent and enthusiasm. His conversation was as professional as the skill which he had demonstrated so superbly throughout the meal. Everything about his food is exciting, original and good. There were no short cuts – everything was there and the result was total enjoyment of a selection of fresh ingredients perfectly planned, prepared and presented – the true mark of a professional. Long may David Everitt-Matthias and his team remain in Cheltenham!

One of my restaurant reviews for Gloucestershire & Avon Life

"<u>From a Cotswold Kitchen</u>"

by

Mo Smith

"<u>Carefree Holiday Catering</u>"

Self catering holidays have increased in popularity over the past decade. Camping and caravan sites at home and abroad have become a familiar part of the landscape in summer. It can be a most relaxing way of taking a holiday especially for families and is usually less expensive than an hotel. Increased trade has brought better facilities. It is possible to hire a fully equipped tent in situ. Spacious caravans fitted with all mod.cons. are available on well planned sites often providing a games room, a swimming pool and a well stocked shop. Cottages and holiday flats have such essentials as washing machines, dishwashers and deep freezers.

The major disadvantage, which most of the family fails to see in the excitement of planning the holiday, is that we still have to eat and if the cook, usually Mother, is to survive this ordeal a little pre-planning is necessary. Holiday activities, leisurely or otherwise induce hunger pains and the smooth running of the kitchen is essential if the holiday is to be enjoyed by everyone.

Experience has taught me to "go prepared". Modern food containers such as ice boxes and freezer bags make transporting food easy and safe and as our holidays are usually taken in this country I insist the car is filled with extra food rather than extra clothes which are usually not needed anyway. Amongst these food boxes there must be a good selection of everyday commodities. Shelf items which are taken for granted at home but are so essential in the preperation of quick substantial meals must be taken if endless shopp ing is to be avoided. Under this heading I include flour, salt and pepper and dried herbs. Chutney and jam, tomato puree and tinned tomatoes. Condensed soups, dried apricots, a selection of nuts and an ample supply of rice and pasta to substitute for potatoes.

My family is of the opinion that unless one good meat and two veg. meal is provided each day, whatever the weather, they have not eaten. On the understanding that someone else gets breakfast and we eat a simple bread and cheese and fruit lunch, I agree to cook a hearty supp er and pudding. In order to keep this promise I decide a little time spent in my own kitchen prior to leaving will pay dividends. This is where being a cook has it's advantages and I use all my skills to plan a few meals which can be prepared in advance and reheated or quickly assembled and served from simple ingredients.

First impressions are important and included in this pre-holiday cooking will be a huge steak and kidney pie to reheat for supper the first evening. This will ease any tension which might have built up on the journey and hopefully it will soften the blow when I announce that washing up is a chore the cook opts out of on holiday.

- 1 -

introducing ... "a touch of originality"

by

Mo Smith

Cooking has fascinated me since childhood and over the past few years I have spent most of my time experimenting, demonstrating, writing and talking about it.

It is an art which can give enjoyment to everyone if tackled with a sense of adventure and fun rather than a chore necessary to keep the body functioning, as is sadly and all too often the case.

Furthermore, unlike any other art, it offers many challenges but with greater rewards the bovious one being that you can actually eat the result of your labours.

Personally, I never cease to be amazed at the numerous dishes which can be created merely by juggling with a few simple, everyday ingredients. Let me illustrate my point a little more clearly by listing a handful of ingredients which are likely to be found in all kitchens - fat, flour, sugar, eggs, milk and water. By varying the quantities used and the initial preperation, many different dishes can be served, each providing it's own individual flavour. For example, Yorkshire pudding; the more substantial family favourite, toad in the hole or delicate wafer thin crepes. For a sweeter tooth a traditional Victoria sandwich or, often more acceptable because of it's fat free content, a Swiss roll; home-made sponge fingers - a treat indeed. Then there are the numerous pastries - shortcrust, puff, choux or one of the many rich flan pastries introduced to us by the French. The list is endless.

Of course to complete the presentation additional ingredients are needed and it is the careful choice and use of these which provides that all important "touch of originality". It does not have to be extravagant or sophisticated. It might be a grating of nutmeg on the freshly cooked sprouts, a dash of curry powder stirred into a rice salad, a teaspoon of horseradish sauce added to savoury eggs or a spoon of marmalade included in the ingredients for a Victoria sandwich. Once the art of combining flavours and textures is mastered cooking becomes sheer joy.

My recipe for spinach roulade provides another example. It uses all the ingredients listed above plus the obvious extras, but the further addition of a little apple purée results in a delicious and memorable balance of flavours. Served hot or cold with a fresh tomato side salad it provides a substantial family meal and if you are attempting to introduce new flavours into your diet it is a good beginning. I do hope you will try it.

Mo Smith

from:
Mo Smith, Bear House, Bisley, Stroud, Glos. GL6 7BB (Glos. 770298)

What Lazy Cook recipes are all about – a brief synopsis

by Lazy Cook Mo Smith

The use of fresh, seasonal ingredients is at the forefront of my recipe development.

I believe there are thousands of people who eat an unhealthy diet, mostly of ready-made meals, because they do not know how to prepare and cook many of the fresh ingredients on sale, they are, in a strange way, fearful of them.

People generally are unaware of the balance of nutrients needed for a healthy diet most of which come from fresh seasonal ingredients.

They believe cooking at home means lots of hard work, time consuming and expensive.

When they get home they want a meal quickly and this is where my Lazy Cook recipes come into their own illustrating how to mix and match the abundance of ready-prepared ingredients with fresh foods to provide a healthy, balanced meal in 'mo-ments'.

For example – 'take one large ready-cooked chicken' – add a handful of other ingredients, and prepare 5 healthy meals for 2 people – that's Lazy Cooking!

My Lazy Cook recipes are increasingly popular because they show how to get the best out of ingredients in the simplest way for healthy home cooking.

S/S 21.3.8~~5~~

Highlights from the shopping basket

Well, we all thought winter was on it's way out and we'd seen

the last of the snow until next year - how mistaken we were ~~because~~

~~last weekend the winter returned - with a vengence -~~ _{but} ~~and~~ the one

person I'm always pleased to see around ^{especially in bad weather} ~~when I let the cat out~~ is

the friendly milkman - how do they do it I always ask myself ~~but~~ ^{and}

what a wonderful service they give in all weathers - so please,

please be kind to your milkman - what would we do without him -

my shopping bags are/~~full~~ ^{heavy} enough without having to carry <u>many</u>

daily pintas - the milkman is all part of our British way of life

isn't he - and it's more <u>British</u> goods the producers are promoting

at the moment and many British grown products are/~~going to~~ ^{being} displaye~~d~~ ^{will}

a special label so that those ~~of us~~ who want to buy as much

British produce as <s>we</s> ^{they} can can be sure we're doing this because of

these special Buy British labels - it applies to fruit, vegetables,

meat, poultry, bacon and cheese - my hope is that it will keep

the standard of British/ ^{produce} up - and we will get more good quality

~~British produce.~~

And the best ~~of the~~ British produce I found yesterday ~~is~~ was

^{at} ~~from~~ the fishmonger and the greengrocer and I'll begin with the

greengrocer where I bought some excellent quality spring cabbage

and some marvellously cheap mushrooms - those lovely large dark

flat ones which give soups and sauces and casserols a wonderful

rich flavour or are equally delicious served on toast - what I call

an "<u>instant</u> tea". But the choice of "Brisish" produce at the

greengrocer is a little limited at the moment - yes, because of

the weather. and Now if you're fed up with frozen ~~and~~ peas and fresh

carrots ~~at the moment~~ because everything else seems pour in quality

or too expensive, just take a closer look at beetroot~~s~~ - the uncooked

ones. Maybe you only think of eating beetroot with salad but it

is really good cooked, and this week I've decided to include on my

recipe sheet my own recipe for "Bisley Beets" - it's slices of

- 2 -

cooked beetroots served with an easy to make sauce using a little
water or stock, a little chutney, French mustard, brown sugar and
vinegar.   You will find uncooked beetroots at between 12 and 15p a
pound so as I said it's worth taking a second look at it and giving
the family a new vegetable course,   Simmer the beetroots for
about 2hrs. depending on their size, peel them as they cool, then
they will store them in the fridge until you want to use them.
Still with the vegetables, there were some excellent courgettes and around yesterday
though they were priced at 65p a pound I decided to buy just one
which cost me 45p.   With this I shall make another tasty vegetable course
possibly use some of those excellent mushrooms and perhaps a few
onion rings - it's an idea you might like to try.

   But one of the real luxuries around at the moment are
Strawberries - these were between 50 and 70p a half pound punnet
yesterday and the quality looked good too - the very sight of
them made me think of hot summer days and teas outside.

   And there were more tastes of summer at the fishmonger but
I'll tell you more about that after the break.

                        before the break
   Well as I said earlier summer really was in the air yesterday,
following the strawberries at the greengrocers you'll never guess
what I saw at the fishmongers - beautiful fresh Scotch salmon cutlets,
but wait for it, they were 4.95p per pound - I did't dare buy any
though it immediately reminded me of a economical recipe I often serve in the
summer when salmon is a little less expensive and I'll remember to
give you more details of that later in the year.   Well, from the
sublime to the rediculous - I bought yesterday smoked haddock at a more
realistic price of 1.59p.   And with this I made the recipe which
I give also you this week and which I call "Easter" Haddock Cream.   All you do
is pop the haddock fillets into hot water for a couple of minutes

188

- 3 -

and as it cool

drain off the liquid and as the fish cools remove all the skin and

any bones, and break the haddock into pieces. Heat two tablespoons
            then

of thick white sauce with a quarter of a pint of single cream,

one teaspoon horseradish cream and a little pepper, add the

pieces of haddock to this sauce and bring to simmer. To serve

this, arrange some cooked rice around a large serving plate or
                                    this
dish (and I usually colour this/yellow) Pour the fish and sauce

in the middle and if you have any, sprinkle with freshly chopped

parsley. And to make this dish even better, I surround the

fish with some manderin orange segments - they add more colour

and flavour, or you could use up some of those egg yolks which
                    alre
you may have/remaining from making meringues - hard boil these,

chop them and arrange them around the fish.

So if you're looking for a new fish dish for Easter, why not
    my Easter Haddock   with useful tips
try this - you can get the complete recipe and the my recipe

for 'Bisley Beets.' by calling at Severn Sound reception or

by sending in a stamped addressed envelope - Bye.

Recipes

Boxing Day Pudding	192
Chicken and Artichoke Salad	193
Chocolate Battenburg Cake	194
Chocolate Bomb	196
Chocolate Orange Sticks	198
The 'Smith family' Christmas Puddings	199
Crystallized Orange Peel	201
Crystallized Pineapple	203
Fish in Batter with Tomato Sauce	206
Gravy	208
Morello Cherry Jam	209
Pineapple Chocolates	211
Quick Cauliflower Cheese	212
Savoury Gateau	213
Tarte Tatin	214
Watercress and Cherry Tomato Salad	216

BOXING DAY PUDDING

Cold Christmas pudding slices
Brandy
425ml (15fl.oz) milk
1 teas. vanilla essence
3 large eggs

Set oven at gas 3/160°C/140°C fan/Aga simmering oven.
Put the pudding slices into a shallow ovenproof dish and
sprinkle liberally with brandy. Put the milk and vanilla
essence into a pan to warm.
Whisk the eggs and sieve into the milk, stir, then pour
over the pudding slices.
Bake, uncovered, in the pre-set oven until set.
Serve from the oven with single cream.

CHICKEN AND ARTICHOKE SALAD – to serve 6–8 persons

Although I have not eaten artichokes as prepared by Ra since the memorable lunch, I do use artichoke hearts regularly and this recipe, which I mostly serve in summer, is a favourite, especially when I am able to buy chargrilled artichoke hearts. Very quick to assemble especially if you buy a large ready cooked chicken.

Cover a large serving plate with shredded lettuce. Arrange overlapping slices of cooked chicken around and fill the centre with artichoke hearts. Finally, immediately before serving, scatter with mustard cress for instant eye-catching presentation.

CHOCOLATE BATTENBURG CAKE – cuts 8–10 slices

For the cake –
175g (6oz) unsalted butter – soften
225g (8oz) caster sugar
3 large eggs – lightly whisk together
225g (8oz) plain flour
2 rounded teas. baking powder
3fl oz single cream
2 rounded teas. cocoa powder

For the Chocolate Almond Paste –
200g (7oz) ground almonds
100g (4oz) icing sugar
100g (4oz) caster sugar
2 rounded teas. cocoa powder
1 small egg
2 spots almond essence
$1/2$ teas. vanilla essence
1 desst. brandy
1 desst. lemon juice
Chocolate Spread

Set oven at gas 4/180°C/160°C fan/Aga baking oven.
Line the ends and base of a 2lb loaf tin with a strip of greaseproof paper and lightly oil. Lightly oil the sides also.
Using a large basin and electric hand whisk, whisk the butter and sugar until light and fluffy. Add the eggs, flour, baking powder and cream and stir together until smooth.
Spread 1/3rd of the mixture to cover the base of the prepared tin.
Put 1/3rd of the mixture on to a plate and stir in the cocoa powder. Put this to cover the mixture in the tin then

cover with the remaining mixture.

Before putting it into the pre-set oven trail a skewer in the shape of a 'Z' lengthways through the mixture to produce a marbled effect. Bake for 30–40mins. or until set – (see Lazy Cook tips).

Remove from oven and loosen the sides of the cooked cake from the tin with a palette knife before removing the cake from the tin and placing it on to a wire tray until cold.

To make the almond paste put the ground almonds, sugars and cocoa powder into a large bowl and stir together.

Put all remaining ingredients (except the chocolate spread), into a jug and whisk together. Pour on to the almond mixture and stir together to a smooth paste.

Remove the paper from the cake and if it has risen cut off the top to make it flat (like a brick).

Using sieved icing sugar, roll out a little of almond paste to fit one side of the cake. Spread the side with chocolate spread before attaching the rolled paste, trim off any surplus. Continue until sides and top of the cake are covered, spreading with chocolate spread as you go.

Squeeze all the edges together between finger and thumb then pinch between little finger to make a crinkly edge.

Using a knife lightly mark the top and sides with diamond shapes.

Lazy Cook tips *– test when the cake is cooked by pressing the centre of the cake and if it bounces back it is set, or put a skewer into the centre and if it comes out clean it is set. The Chocolate Spread I use is 'PlaisirMiel' (a Belgium milk chocolate spread with honey.)*

*'CHOCOLATE BOMB' – a pudding to keep in store –
when I made this for our special celebration party on
31st December 1999, I decorated it with sparklers and
called it 'Sparkling Dome'*

High on my shopping list at Christmas time is an extra pot
of double cream – this will keep fresh much longer than
whipping; it can be made into single cream by stirring in a
little milk; it will thicken a sauce and, should you overbuy,
a 10oz carton can be whipped and used to line a 2pt basin
and then frozen in readiness to make into a Chocolate
Bomb – a stunning pudding which will delight family and
friends especially if it is topped with sparklers and lit for a
dramatic presentation – make it now to keep in store for
Christmas or into the New Year.

Chocolate Bomb – serves 6–8 portions

To be prepared and frozen -
300ml (10fl.oz) double cream
175g (6oz) bitter chocolate
50g (2oz) butter
50g (2oz) walnuts – chopped (optional)
4 large eggs – separated

For decoration –
sparklers or chocolate squares

Whip the cream to a spreadable consistency, stir in 3–4
teas. ready grated chocolate then spread to cover the
inside of a 2pt basin, put into a freezer bag and freeze for at
least 24hrs.
Make the filling by melting the remaining chocolate and

butter together, stir in egg yolks and chopped walnuts.

Using a large bowl, whisk the egg whites to a stiff consistency then stir in the chocolate mixture.

Pour into the frozen cream mould, put back into the freezer bag and freeze for a minimum of 24hrs. or until required.

To serve, remove the freezer bag and put the bomb into a refrigerator to thaw a little before loosening the side with a palette knife and turning on to a serving dish.

Leave in a refrigerator to continue to thaw for 3–4hrs. or until the centre has defrosted (test with a metal skewer).

Before serving, pipe with whipped cream (optional), spike with chocolate squares and top with sparklers.

Lazy Cook tips – *small sparklers especially produced for serving for food presentation can be purchased from specialist shops – keep a supply in store.*

CHOCOLATE ORANGE STICKS

Crystallized orange peel (recipe page 201)
Bitter chocolate – melted

Cut the peel into strips using scissors and dip each strip into melted bitter chocolate. Remove with a fork and shake off any surplus chocolate before placing the coated strips on to foil and leaving to set.
Store, on the foil, in a box.

THE 'SMITH FAMILY' CHRISTMAS PUDDINGS
– makes 3 x 1kg (2lb) puddings – fun for all the family to make, stir and wish!

300g (12oz) raisins
300g (12oz) sultanas
300g (12oz) currants
200g (8oz) dark cane sugar
150g (6oz) mixed peel
150g (6oz) fresh breadcrumbs – brown or white
300g (12oz) grated suet
150g (6oz) plain flour
1 teas. mixed spice
300g (12oz) grated cooking apple
50g (2oz) flaked almonds – browned
1 small carrot – grated
zest of 1 lemon
5 large eggs – whisk together
3oz brandy
50g (2oz) butter
100g (4oz) whole almonds with skins

Spread the butter thickly on to the base of 3 1kg (2lb) pudding basins and press the whole almonds into it.

Mix all reamining ingredients together and pack into the prepared basins.

Cover with buttered greaseproof paper then foil (each pleated in the middle), and tie with string.

To steam the puddings (this can be done overnight)

Set oven at gas 3/160°C/140°C fan/Aga simmering oven.

Stand the filled basins in a large roasting tin and pour in a kettle of boiling water.

Cover with foil and put into the pre-set oven for 6–8hrs.

or until the puddings are dark in colour (top up with more boiling water if necessary).

Allow to cool before removing from the basins and wrapping in greaseproof and foil in readiness for re-heating on Christmas day.

Lazy Cook tips *– steaming in the oven avoids staying in the kitchen all day to top up saucepans with boiling water, and a kitchen full of steam. On Christmas day put the pudding, in the parcel in which it has been stored, into a medium oven for several hours or until hot throughout. Friends with microwaves tell me puddings can be heated in these – follow the manufacturers instructions.*

CRYSTALLIZED ORANGE PEEL

Peel from 4–6 large oranges
Granulated sugar
Water

Carefully remove and discard the white pith from the orange skins using a sharp knife.

Put the prepared peel into a saucepan, cover with cold water, bring to a boil then reduce to a simmer, put lid on pan and simmer for 30 mins.

Strain off the cooking liquid into a measuring jug. Put the peel on to a plate.

Make a syrup as follows –

Allow 35g (1$^1/_2$oz) sugar to each fruit and 1 tablespoon cooking liquid to each 25g (1oz) sugar, i.e.

6 oranges = 250g (9oz) sugar = 9 tbls. cooking liquid

Dissolve the required amount of sugar into the cooking liquid by bringing it slowly to the boil stirring continually.

When the sugar has complete dissolved (when there is no gritty sound when the base of the pan is prodded with a wooded spoon), add the peel, bring to a simmer and simmer, uncovered, for 30 mins.

If the syrup becomes too thick or reduces before the cooking time is up add a little fresh water.

Using kitchen tongs remove the peel from the syrup and put to dry overnight on a wire tray placed over a swiss roll tin to catch the drips.

Next day roll each piece of peel in granulated sugar and store in an airtight jar – use within 3 months.

Lazy Cook tips – *the remaining syrup has a bitter taste and I have not as yet found a use for it. The crystallized peel can be cut up and used in, or to decorate cakes, or, favourite of all, to make Chocolate Orange Sticks.*

CRYSTALLIZED PINEAPPLE

I have crystallized various whole fruits over the years but the one I find easiest and the most successful is pineapple. Although at first glance it may seem a complicated process it really isn't and requires just a few minutes of your time each day, for a few days – my original comments under 'Preparation Time' reads as follows – "about 15mins. for the initial preparation and 5mins. each day for 13 days". The crystallized fruit can be added to cake mixtures, stirred into ice-cream or, best of all, made into chocolates. I recommend you begin the process not later than 1st December.

Ingredients –
1 large fresh pineapple – must not be over ripe or bruised
water
granulated sugar

Preparation –
Cut off the top and the end of the pineapple and discard.
Stand the pineapple on its end and cut off and discard the spiky skin then remove and discard any bits which remain in the pineapple using the point of a potato peeler.
Turn the skinned pineapple on its side and slice into rings not less than 1cm ($^1/_2$") in thickness.
Remove and discard the centre stalk from each ring (this is best done using a small plain pastry cutter or a serrated knife).
Weigh and record the weight of the pineapple rings before placing them in a saucepan, pour over sufficient boiling water to cover.

Bring to a boil, reduce to a simmer and simmer, without lid, for 2–3mins. or until the pineapple is just tender – it must not overcook.

Strain off the cooking liquid into a measuring jug and keep. Put the pineapple into a large basin.

Make a syrup as follows –

To each 450g (1lb) pineapple allow 300ml (10oz) cooking liquid and add to this 175g (6oz) granulated sugar. Dissolve the sugar in the measured water and bring to the boil then pour it over the pineapple rings and leave for 24hrs (when cool cover with foil).

It is important at this point to record each day, and the date, and the foregoing is Day 1.

Day 2 – Drain the syrup from the pineapple into a saucepan, stir in 50g (2oz) sugar until it is dissolved then bring the syrup to a boil. Pour back over the pineapple and leave for 24hrs.

Days 3–6 Repeat the process for Day 2.

Day 7 – Add 75g (3oz) sugar to the syrup and when dissolved add the pineapple rings, bring to the boil and boil for 4mins. Pour back into the basin and leave for 48hrs.

Day 9 – Repeat the process for Day 7 then leave for 4 days.

Day 13 – Lift the pineapple from the syrup on to a wire tray placed over a swiss roll tin, or similar, to catch the drips. Put to dry for several days in a 'very low' oven, possibly with the door slightly ajar to keep the temperature down* turning the rings over from time to time. When no longer sticky the fruit is ready to be stored in a box lined with waxed paper (from a cereal box). Store in a cool, dry place. It is best used with 2 months.

*other 'drying' places are an airing cupboard or on a central heating boiler.

The remaining syrup can be boiled to setting point – test by putting a little on to a plate and when cold push your finger through the centre and it is set if the channel does not close.

Pour into clean hot jars and seal with a disc of greaseproof paper and a metal lid. Use to top tarts and cakes, to spread on to bread and butter, or to pour over ice cream.

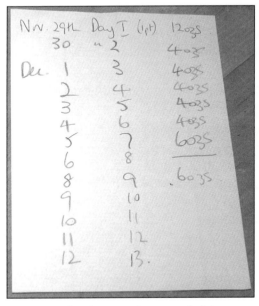

Crystallized Pineapple – recorded days

FISH IN BATTER WITH TOMATO SAUCE
– makes approx. 12

150ml (5fl.oz) batter mixture
225g (8oz) cooked prawns
little oil

Make the batter a good half hour in advance of cooking.
Set oven at gas 6/200°C/180°C fan/Aga roasting oven, 2nd runner down.
Using a 12 hole patti tin, pour a little oil into each hole and put in the pre-set oven for 1–2mins. or until hot.
Whisk a tablespoon of cold water into the batter mixture and pour it into each hole then drop a few prawns into each.
Return to the oven and bake for 10–15mins. or until well risen and golden.
Serve directly from the oven piled on to a hot dish/es.
Serve the hot sauce separately.

Lazy Cook tips *– these are so quick to make and make an excellent starter. The fish fillings an be varied. To serve as a dessert, add apple, peach or plum slices and serve hot with a little icing sugar sieved on top.*

<u>Batter Mixture</u>
300ml (10oz) milk
100g (4oz) plain flour
2 large egg
2tbls. cold water

Set oven at gas 6/200°C/180°C fan/Aga roasting oven.

Put the milk into a food processor (or liquidizer) before adding the flour and eggs.

Process for a few seconds until smooth.

Pour into a jug, cover and put into a refrigerator or cold larder for 30mins. to 1 hour.

Whisk in the cold water before cooking as directed in recipe.

Lazy Cook tips – *I use this recipe when making Yorkshire pudding to serve with roast beef. I always stand a joint for roasting on a trivet in the roasting tin and this allows me to pour the Yorkshire pudding mixture into the tin beneath the joint (at the time estimated to cook the pudding, this may be after the joint is cooked to your liking). Cut the cooked pudding into wedges and place around the joint. You will find everybody wants the slightly 'soggy' pudding into which the juices from the roasting joint have drained – British cooking at its best!*

<u>Tomato Sauce</u>
Tomato ketchup
Fresh lemon juice
Sundried tomato paste
Runny honey

To each tablespoon tomato ketchup add one teaspoon sundried tomato paste and one teaspoon fresh lemon juice. Stir over a gentle heat until hot. Taste and if too sharp sweeten with a little runny honey. Serve hot or cold.

GRAVY – *to serve with a roast*

Blend 1–2tbls. plain flour to a smooth paste with cold water and add to the juices in the roasting tin (once the cooked joint and the trivet have been removed).
Add a few spots of gravy browning and a little stock, wine or water and stir over a hot heat until it boils.
Thin down to the required consistency by adding more stock or water and simmer until needed – serve hot.

Lazy Cook tips – *if the juices in the pan are too fatty, tilt the pan and spoon out any excess fat before adding the gravy ingredients. The amount of flour used will depend on the thickness of the gravy preferred. More wine, or cream can be added. Any leftover gravy should be stored, covered, in a refrigerator or cold larder and used for making a Shepherds or Cottage pie, or added to soup.*

MORELLO CHERRY JAM

Friends in the village have a morello cherry tree which bears fruit each year at a time when they are on holiday. Angela very kindly suggests that I pick them. This year the crop has been exceptionally good and when walking past their house one day I noticed the tree laden with plump dark cherries, I just had to pick them. Within a short time I picked 8lbs – and left some for the birds. These were too precious a crop to freeze, they went straight into the preserving pan and made eight pounds of delicious jam.

4kg (8lbs) morello cherries
2¹/₂kg (5¹/₂lbs) sugar
2 rounded teas. citric acid

Wash the fruit. Put a little water in the pan to prevent sticking, add the fruit and simmer until it has softened.
Stir in the sugar and citric acid until it has all dissolved. Bring to a rapid boil and boil until a setting point is reached (10–15mins). Remove stones.
Pour jam into hot clean jars, top with a disc of greaseproof paper and seal with a metal lid.
Label and store in a cool, dark place.

Lazy Cook tips *– if you have a tool for removing fruit stones I suggest you use that before softening the fruit. Put the stones into a bag and put the bag into the pan with the fruit. Remove them before rapidly boiling.*

To test for a set – after the recommended time for rapid

boiling, remove the pan from the heat and put a little jam on to a plate and leave until it becomes cold and a skin forms. Push a finger through the centre to make a channel and if this does not close the jam is set. If the channel closes, bring the jam back to a rapid boil and test every 1–2mins. until a set is reached.

PINEAPPLE CHOCOLATES

Crystallized pineapple rings (recipe page 203)
Bitter chocolate – melted
Foil

Break the chocolate into a basin and melt in a slow oven
or a microwave.
Cut each ring of crystallized pineapple into chocolate sized
pieces and dip in the melted chocolate.
Remove using a fork and place on foil until the chocolate
has set.
Store, on the foil, in a box.
Peel from foil to serve.

QUICK CAULIFLOWER CHEESE – to serve 4–6

1 cauliflower – medium sized
100g (4oz) grated cheese (a mixture of Stilton and Cheddar)
50g (2oz) jumbo oats

Break the cauliflower into small florets and wash.

Add to a pan containing a little boiling water and boil, with lid on pan, for 2–3mins. or until it just begins to soften.

Using a slotted spoon put into a shallow, ovenproof dish and add 3–4tbls. of the cooking liquid.

Mix the cheeses and oats together and put on top of the cauliflower.

Brown under a hot grill or in the oven (gas 6/200°C/ 180°C fan/Aga roasting oven) until the cheese has softened and the oats are browning.

Lazy Cook tips – *always cook vegetables in the minimum amount of boiling water. The cauliflower can be cooked and stored, covered, in a refrigerator until it is needed – use within 3 days. Breadcrumbs can be used instead of oats.*

SAVOURY GATEAU – *to serve 8–10 slices*

1 x $^{1}/_{2}$kg (1lb) loaf of a cob shape – brown or white
50g (2oz) butter or margarine – softened
175g (6oz) meat paté
175g (6oz) fish paté
225g (8oz) cream or curd cheese
a little single cream or milk
freshly ground white pepper

Suggested garnish –
tomato, orange and lime slices
spring onions – green stalk end
radishes
watercress

Remove all the crusts from the loaf before slicing it horizontally into 3 slices of equal thickness.
Spread each slice with butter and sandwich together with the paté so that it looks like one big thick sandwich, place it on to a serving dish.
Soften the cheese with a little cream or milk and season with freshly ground white pepper and cover the loaf with this.
Garnish as in the picture.

Lazy Cook tips – *this is a most eye-catching creation. It can be made to the 'big sandwich' stage and frozen until needed – make sure it is thoroughly thawed before covering with cheese by piercing with a skewer. It is very popular with vegetarians if made using acceptable fillings – a great recipe for party time.*

TARTE TATIN – which cuts into 6 portions
Translated from the recipe dictated by Armide

700–900g (1$\frac{1}{2}$–2lb) dessert apples
50g (2oz) unsalted butter
50g (2oz) caster sugar

For the pâte brisée –
100g (4oz) plain flour
50g (2oz) unsalted butter
25g (1oz) caster sugar
1 egg yolk
1 desst. cold water

I find the easiest and quickest way to make this is to mix it in a food processor as follows (see Lazy Cook tips for traditional method).

Put the flour and sugar into the processor and process together for a few seconds.
Add the butter (cut into pieces as you add it), egg yolk and water and process until the mixture forms a ball.

To make the tart –
Peel and core the apples and cut into slices.
Use a round enamel, or similar pan, that can be used on a hob and then in the oven.
Lightly spread the base of the pan with butter and top with a little of the sugar.
Cover with apple slices, nicely arranged, then add pats of butter and sugar and remaining apple slices in layers until all ingredients are used.

Put the pan on a hob, or over a flame, until the ingredients begin to caramelise (approx. 15mins. on a medium heat). Remove pan from heat.

Set oven at gas 6/200°C/180°C fan/Aga roasting oven (highest runner).

Make the pâte brisée and roll it out to fit the top of the pan (like a lid).

Bake in the pre-set oven for 10mins. or until the pastry is biscuit in colour.

Turn on to a hot plate and serve hot, warm or cold with single cream (optional).

Lazy Cook tips – *I often make this using Bramley apples which produce an excellent flavour but they do not retain their shape as dessert apples do. Most recipes recommend that pastries are made then stored in a refrigerator or larder before rolling. If I do this I find the pastry is then too cold to roll and so I roll it as soon as it is made.*

To make pâte brisée using the traditional method –
Put the flour and sugar on to a board and mix together then make a well in the centre.
Add the butter pieces, egg yolk and water and mix together using the fingertips of one hand and when blended work in the flour. Using the 'heel' of the hand knead it into a smooth ball of paste.

WATERCRESS AND CHERRY TOMATO SALAD

When Liz came to pick up my manuscript for proof-reading she brought me several bunches of watercress fresh from Alresford. To this I added a handful of freshly picked cherry tomatoes from the hanging basket outside my kitchen door, and with the addition of a few other ingredients I made a delicious salad – a fine example of fresh ingredients served simply to produce the best flavours – healthy eating doesn't get better.

Wash and spin dry some watercress and put into a salad bowl.
Top with cherry tomatoes, several spring onions thinly sliced, radishes cut into halves, a few uneven slices cucumber, a handful of seedless grapes and a light vinaigrette.

Tip of the Month Recipes

The following are examples of my Tip of the Month recipes. I sent these as a Press Release by email, to the media. All the recipes are taken from my Lazy Cook books.

Aubergine – Baked Aubergine	218
Beetroot – Bisley Beets	219
Bread Pudding – Bread Pudding with an Orange and Ginger Wine Sauce	220
Fish Pie – Fish and Bacon Pie	221
Food for Free – Bramble Meringue Pie	221
Lemons – Summer Liver	222
Mustard Pickle – Pickled Pork	223
Oranges – Hot Orange Pudding	224
Oven Chips – Village Pie	225
Pears – Dessert Pear with Smoked Salmon and Peppered Cream	226
Rhubarb – Rhubarb Jelly with Raspberry Cream	227
Soup – Tangy Tomato Soup	228
Vegetable Marrow (or overgrown courgettes) Marrow and Tomato Bake	229

AUBERGINE

This richly coloured vegetable can be served in so many ways and because of its high protein content it provides a perfectly balanced meal without the addition of fish, meat or poultry. Baked Aubergine is just one way I serve it for a delicious lunch or supper – I hope you will enjoy it.

Baked Aubergine – to serve 2

Set oven at gas 6/200°C/400°F/Aga roasting oven, 3rd runner down. Wash and top and tail one large aubergine and cut in half lengthways. Remove the flesh and keep. Score the flesh side of the skins and brush (and the skin), with oil before placing them, skin side down, in a shallow ovenproof dish and bake in the pre-set oven for 10–15mins. or until the skin has softened. Meanwhile prepare the filling by adding one medium onion – chopped, to a pan containing a little boiling water or stock, place lid on pan and cook until the onion begins to soften. Cut the reserved aubergine flesh into small cubes and add to the softened onion. Add also, 100g (4oz) chopped mushrooms, 1 teaspoon mushroom ketchup, 1 teaspoon sundried tomato paste and freshly ground pepper, stir, and cook for 2–3mins. or until the aubergine begins to soften, with lid on pan – (a little vegetable stock or water may need to be added to prevent sticking). Stir in 4–6 sun dried tomatoes (cut into strips), and several good pinches dried mixed herbs. Remove the aubergine cases from the oven and pack with the prepared filling. Mix 2 tablespoons fresh or dried breadcrumbs with 50g (2oz) grated cheese of a good flavour and put on top. Return to the oven and bake, uncovered, for 10–15mins.

or until the topping is crisp and brown. Serve hot with rice or salad.

Lazy Cook tip – *I find a grapefruit knife a useful tool for removing aubergine flesh.*

BEETROOT

Now is the time to buy new season's beetroots, they are small and tender and if you are able to buy them by the bunch with good leafy tops, these can be washed and cooked and eaten as for spinach. Small beetroots can be cooked whole – cover with cold water and simmer for about an hour. When cold discard the peel and serve the beetroots whole dressed with a little oil and vinegar and scattered with tarragon, fresh or dried. Alternatively, serve the cooked beetroots as a vegetable as in my recipe for 'Bisley Beets' as follows –

Bisley Beets – serves 4–6

Skin and slice 2 large cooked beetroots into a shallow ovenproof dish. Skin and slice one large onion and soften in approx. 100ml/4fl.oz boiling water with lid on pan. Remove the cooked slices and place on top of the beetroot. To the remaining cooking liquid add 2 tbls. vinegar, 1 tbls. demerera sugar, 1 teas. Dijon mustard and 1 tbls. chutney. Bring to boil and stir over the heat until it reduces. Pour this over the beetroot and onion slices, cover with foil and cook for 15–20mins. or until hot throughout at gas 6/200°C/180°C fan/Aga roasting oven.

BREAD PUDDING

I well remember the bread pudding my mother made and which I loved. My recipe is, I think, equally delicious but, being a Lazy Cook it is much quicker to make and the Ginger Wine Sauce makes it a very special pudding to serve on all occasions.

Bread Pudding with an Orange and Ginger Wine Sauce – serves 6

Heat 100ml (4oz) milk, stir in 1 dessertspoon black treacle and when dissolved add 100g (4oz) fresh breadcrumbs (brown or white), 1 tablespoon marmalade, 25g (1oz) shredded suet, $^1/_2$teas. mixed spice and 100g (4oz) dried apricots – sliced, stir all well. Pack into a lightly oiled pie dish and leave to rest for 15–30mins. Scatter a little demerera sugar on top and bake for 30–40mins. at gas 4/180°C/160°C fan/Aga baking oven. Meanwhile make a ginger wine sauce to serve with the cooked pudding by simmering together the juice and zest of one fresh orange, 1 teas. orange flower water (optional), and 50ml (2oz) ginger wine.

Lazy Cook tip – *for a more eye-catching presentation smear butter over the base of a pie dish, scatter with demerera sugar and arrange the whole apricots on top then cover with the pudding mixture. Bake as directed in the recipe but to serve turn it out on to a hot serving plate. This recipe can also be served as a cake – cut into chunks.*

FISH PIE

This is always a popular meal and can be a good way of making a small amount of fish stretch to serve a number of people. With this in mind I top this particular pie with a mixture of breadcrumbs and bacon which add to the flavours and texture. The following recipe will serve 6 portions.

Fish and Bacon Pie

Set oven at gas 6/200°C/180°C fan/Aga roasting oven. Pour water or white wine to cover the base of a shallow ovenproof dish and top with 450g (1lb) fish fillets, sprinkle with a little fresh lemon juice and scatter with capers and a few seedless grapes. Melt 50g (2oz) butter in a pan over a gentle heat, stir in 50g (2oz) plain flour and mix to a smooth paste. Add 600ml (1pt) fish or vegetable stock or milk (or a mixture), and stir until it boils (add more liquid if necessary to make into a pouring sauce) then stir in a tbls. cream (optional), before seasoning with freshly ground white pepper. Pour over the fish and top with a mixture of breadcrumbs (fresh or dried), chopped parsley and thyme (fresh or dried), and chopped bacon pieces. Bake in the pre-set oven for 15–20mins. or until hot and bubbling throughout. Serve hot or cold with vegetables or salad, and fresh bread.

FOOD FOR FREE

Any time now the hedgerows will be bursting with nuts, sloes and blackberries – all awaiting our picking. Cobnuts and wet walnuts to shell and eat or add to cakes and pud-dings. Sloes to saturate with gin in readiness for Christmas and blackberries, simply delicious washed and served with a little clotted cream, washed and frozen for winter use, or mixed with new seasons Bramley apples and made into my Bramble Meringue Pie as follows –

Bramble Meringue Pie

Set oven at gas 6/200°C/180°C fan/Aga roasting oven. Simmer some fresh blackberries with Bramley apple slices in just enough water to cover the base of the pan. Put lid on pan and cook until they pulp, sweeten with a little runny honey to taste then pour into a ready baked pastry case. Spread the top with meringue made with 2 egg whites whisked until they are of a stiff cottonwool texture then stir in 100g (4oz) caster sugar and a little pink food colouring (optional). Place the filled pastry case on a baking tray and bake in the pre-set oven for 5–10mins. or until the meringue starts to brown. Serve, or reduce oven temperature to gas 3/160°C/130°C fan/Aga simmering oven and continue baking until the meringue becomes crisp or until you wish to serve it. Serve warm or cold with single cream.

LEMONS

Always remove the zest from lemons before slicing or squeezing them, this will keep in a sealed container in the fridge and is then instantly available for scattering into, or onto the top of cakes and puddings, salads and savoury meals, and especially when making my Summer Liver – a 'must' to have in the fridge in readiness to serve as a summer lunch accompanied with salad, warm bread and a bottle of chilled Rosé

Summer Liver – to serve 4
Whilst 1tls. oil is heating in a large sauté or frying pan, dry thin slices of lambs liver (using a minimum of 450g), on kitchen paper before lightly coating in flour seasoned with freshly ground pepper. Add to the hot oil and turn each slice as blood seeps out (approx. 1–2mins.). Remove from pan on to kitchen paper to absorb any excess oil before placing on a hot serving dish. Sprinkle liberally with fresh lemon juice and keep warm. Repeat until all the liver is cooked, scraping the base of the pan and adding a little more oil as necessary to prevent sticking. To serve, scatter the cooked liver with freshly chopped parsley and plenty of lemon zest.

MUSTARD PICKLE

Liquidise or process the contents of a jar of mustard pickle (or piccalilli) and this instantly becomes an invaluable ingredient to keep in store for use as a mustard sauce to serve hot or cold. Stir it into cooked rice or pasta; serve alongside black pudding or slices of bacon or ham, or use to make my Pickled Pork recipe – a delicious meal prepared in minutes

Pickled Pork – to serve 4 portions
Set oven at gas 4/180°C/160°C fan/Aga baking oven.
Trim and discard any fat from 4 shoulder stakes or boneless

pork steaks. Whilst 1tls. oil is heating in a sauté or frying pan, dry the chops on kitchen paper before lightly coating in flour seasoned with freshly ground pepper, add to the hot oil and cook for approx. 1min. on each side to brown, remove from pan. Dab the base of the pan with clean kitchen paper to remove any excess oil, add a little hot water to the pan and scape up all meat sediment which will have stuck to the base. Add approx. half the jar of liquidised mustard pickle (or piccalilli), and a few white cocktail onions (optional), but no vinegar, and thin down with a few tbls. meat or vegetable stock, or water and stir until simmering. Taste and if the sauce is too sharp sweeten by stirring in a little runny honey. Return the steaks to the sauce, spoon some of the sauce over and bring back to a simmer. Cover and cook in the pre-set oven, or on the hob, for 30–40mins. or until the meat is tender, reducing the temperature after 10mins. to prevent the sauce boiling.

ORANGES

No sooner has the turkey soup finished and Seville oranges are on sale, yes, it's marmalade making time. I use marmalade a lot in my recipes and I am reminded of the pudding I make when we celebrate Burns Night with local friends. As with most of my recipes it can be assembled in minutes using store-cupboard ingredients and the result is a pudding full of good flavours, I hope you will try it.

Hot Orange Pudding to serve 4
Defrost a sheet of ready-rolled puff pastry, grease the rim of

a shallow pie dish with oil or fat. Put 4 tablespoons orange marmalade into the dish and spread to cover the base. Thinly slice 2 large oranges (including peel), and arrange these, overlapping, over the marmalade (discard all pips). Place the pastry over the dish and press down on the rim before trimming off the surplus. Mark the centre of the pie with a cross and stand it on a baking sheet before putting into a hot oven (gas 7/220°C/200°C fan/Aga roasting oven), and bake for 20–30mins. or until the pastry has risen and is turning to a biscuit colour. Remove from oven and allow to cool slightly before turning it on to a hot, deep, serving dish and serve hot or warm with single cream.

Lazy Cook tip – *take special care when turning the pudding on to the plate because the marmalade, which becomes a sauce, is runny and very hot.*

OVEN CHIPS

Some would say the best thing since sliced bread – and certainly a boon to Lazy Cooks. I use them mostly to top pies of the Shepherds and Cottage varieties – both delicious meals to eat but oh what a time it takes to prepare when the topping involves cooking potatoes then slicing or mashing – and all that extra washing up! Ring the changes and make my Village Pie which I can assure you will go down a treat, especially with the kids.

Village Pie – serves 4–6
Set oven at gas 6/200°C/180°C fan/Aga roasting oven.

Soften a large chopped onion in a little boiling water. Add 450g (1lb) minced beef, break it down with a fork and cook over a gentle heat for 5–10mins. stirring from time to time. Stir in 225g (8oz) chicken livers, 1 x 400g tin chopped tomatoes, pinch of sugar, 2fl.oz red or white wine (or stock), freshly ground black pepper, mixed herbs (fresh or dried), and simmer with lid on pan for 5–10mins. or until the contents have blended together. Pour into a shallow ovenproof dish and top with oven chips straight from the freezer. Stand the dish on a baking tray and cook in the pre-set oven for 20–30mins. until the chips begin to brown and all the ingredients are hot and bubbling.

PEARS

The autumn brings new seasons pears – the fruit with a pearly-white flesh and a nutty flavour – the prima donna of all fruits which dictates just when it should be eaten. As I tentatively cut into a pear I am reminded of the little girl who had a little curl right in the middle of her forehead – when she was good she was very very good but when she was bad she was horrid! One of my favourite ways of serving pears is as a starter or light meal with smoked salmon and a peppered cream – a delicious combination of flavours.

Dessert Pear with Smoked Salmon and Peppered Cream
Skin a pear and cut in half lengthways. Remove the stalk and fill the cavity with peppered Boursin cream cheese then place, cut side down, on to individual serving plates. Cover each pear with strips of smoked salmon and top

with a curled fresh anchovy, (or a thin slice of lemon). Heat any remaining Boursin in a pan with a little milk and stir to make it into a sauce which can be trailed round each pear half. Serve with slices of wholemeal bread and butter, and salad.

RHUBARB

The first of our own fruits and a reminder that summer is on its way. As a child I used to pull a slender young stick from the garden, dip the tip in sugar and eat it – I can taste it now – happy childhood memories. I was also told that rhubarb should not be eaten after the end of July so enjoy it while you can. I can recommend the following recipe, it's a good way of using up a couple of spoons of stewed rhubarb, and another of our own delicious summer fruits, raspberries.

Rhubarb Jelly with Raspberry Cream
1 pkt raspberry flavoured jelly cubes
2 serving spoons of cooked rhubarb and juice
5 fl.oz double cream
225g (8oz) fresh raspberries

Break the jelly cubes into a measuring jug. Make up to 300ml ($^1/_2$pt) with boiling water and stir until the cubes have dissolved. Stir in the cooked rhubarb and 2 extra serving spoons of rhubarb juice. Make up to 650ml (1pt 2fl.oz) with more boiling water. Pour into a mould or dish and leave to set. To serve, spread the jelly with whipped cream and top with raspberries.

Lazy Cook tips – *a jelly packed with good fruit flavours and ideal for summer serving. Can be made using gelatine crystals or leaf gelatine – follow the manufacturer's instructions to make up.*

SOUP

Jack Frost is a cummin – according to the weatherman! Winter is the time for comfort food and I can recommend nothing more comforting in cold weather than a bowl of home-made soup. Become squirrel-like and keep in store all you need to make my 'Tangy Tomato Soup' – one of the quickest and most popular soups I make – it will give you a nourishing meal in Mo-ments! – make a batch to keep in a refrigerator or freeze in portion-sized helpings.

Tangy Tomato Soup – to serve 6–8 helpings
Skin and finely chop one large onion, wash and thinly slice 2 carrots and soften these in a little boiling water with lid on pan. Remove with a slotted spoon and process or liquidise with a 600g tin of tomatoes. Return to the pan juices and add 1lt. ham, chicken or vegetable stock (home-made if you have it), 2tbls. orange marmalade, freshly ground white pepper and half a teaspoon of mixed dried herbs. Stir well and simmer for 30mins. with lid on pan. Serve topped with orange zest and/or a swirl of cream – optional. Store, covered, in a fridge and use within 5 days.

VEGETABLE MARROW (or overgrown courgettes)

Marrows are cheap and plentiful in early autumn and can be cooked in so many ways – stuffed marrow is an old favourite, or marrow rings served with various savoury fillings can be served as a starter or light meal, but for a really quick recipe to serve as a vegetable course or, accompanied with bread, rice or couscous as a vegetarian meal I recommend my Marrow and Tomato Bake

Marrow and Tomato Bake

Set oven at gas 6/450°F/220°C/Aga roasting oven. Top and tail a marrow, cut into quarter strips lengthways and remove and discard centre seeds. Cut each strip into mouthsized pieces and cook in boiling water for a minute. Remove from pan with a slotted spoon and put into a shallow ovenproof dish. Season with chopped sage (fresh or dried) then top with a tin of chopped tomatoes and season with freshly ground black pepper and a sprinkling of sugar. Grate a mixture of Cheddar and Stilton cheeses and mix with a roughly equal quantity of breadcrumbs (fresh or dried), or jumbo oats, and cover the tomatoes with this. Bake in the pre-set oven for 15–20mins. or until the cheesy crust is browning and the ingredients are hot throughout – serve immediately or reduce oven temperature to it keep warm until needed for serving.

Index

Introduction   1

Part 1 – A Bee in my Bonnet   3

Part 2 – From Cooker to Computer   103

Features   179

Recipes   191

Tip of the Month Recipes   217